GREEK
TRAGEDIES

VOLUME

1

W9-APE-148

AESCHYLUS

AGAMEMNON
Translated by Richmond Lattimore

PROMETHEUS BOUND
Translated by David Grene

SOPHOCLES

OEDIPUS THE KING
Translated by David Grene

ANTIGONE
Translated by David Grene

EURIPIDES

HIPPOLYTUS
Translated by David Grene

GREEK
TRAGEDIES

Edited by

DAVID GRENE *and* RICHMOND LATTIMORE

VOLUME

1

Second Edition

THE UNIVERSITY OF CHICAGO PRESS

CHICAGO & LONDON

THE UNIVERSITY OF CHICAGO PRESS, CHICAGO 60637
THE UNIVERSITY OF CHICAGO PRESS, LTD., LONDON

Introduction © 1960 by Richmond Lattimore

Agamemnon © 1947 by Richmond Lattimore, © 1953 by The
  University of Chicago

Prometheus Bound © 1942, 1991 by The University of Chicago

Oedipus the King © 1942 by The University of Chicago

Antigone © 1991 by The University of Chicago

Hippolytus © 1942 by The University of Chicago

All rights reserved.
Second edition published 1991 by The University of Chicago Press
Printed in the United States of America
00 99 98 97 96 95 94 93
10 9 8 7 6 5 4 3

Library of Congress Cataloging-in-Publication Data

Greek tragedies / edited by David Grene and Richmond Lattimore.
  —2nd ed.
      p. cm.
    Translated from Greek.
    Selections from the Greek tragedies published in 1960 by the
  University of Chicago Press.
    ISBN 0–226–30790–5
    1. Greek drama (Tragedy)—Translations into English. 2. English
  drama (Tragedy)—Translations from Greek.   I. Grene, David.   II. Lattimore, Richmond Alexander, 1906-1984.
  PA3626.A2G7 1991
  882'.0108—dc20   90–49984
                                                              CIP

⊗The paper used in this publication meets the minimum require-
ments of the American National Standard for Information Sci-
ences—Permanence of Paper for Printed Library Materials, ANSI
Z39.48–1984.

All rights of performance, professional and amateur, are strictly reserved. Requests for permission should be addressed to the pub-
lisher.

PUBLISHER'S NOTE

In this edition of *Greek Tragedies,* volume 1, Elizabeth Wyckoff's translation of *Antigone* (1954) has been replaced with a new translation by David Grene. Also, David Grene has made some revisions to his translation of *Prometheus Bound.*

Excepting David Grene's translator's notes for *Prometheus Bound* and *Antigone,* the brief introductions to the plays in this volume were written by Richmond Lattimore, who wrote, "As befits a limited volume, I have tried to state, very briefly, the essential features of each tragedy here reprinted. The personal views given are, of course, my own, and the translators, other than myself, are not to be held responsible."

Longer and fuller introductions, mostly by the translators themselves, will be found in *The Complete Greek Tragedies,* edited by David Grene and Richmond Lattimore. The complete collection of Greek tragedies is available in nine paperback volumes. These are listed at the end of this volume.

CONTENTS

AGAMEMNON

Translated by Richmond Lattimore

INTRODUCTION

Agamemnon is the first part of the trilogy known as *The Oresteia*, the other two parts being *The Libation Bearers* and *The Eumenides*. The trilogy was presented in 458 B.C. and won first prize.

According to the legend, in the version used by Aeschylus, Atreus tricked his brother, Thyestes, into devouring his own children, all but one. Thyestes cursed the entire house. In the next generation, Agamemnon and Menelaus, sons of Atreus, were kings in Argos. Helen, wife of Menelaus, fled to Troy with Paris (Alexander). Agamemnon led the expedition to Troy and, to insure its success, sacrificed his daughter, Iphigeneia, to Artemis. Clytaemestra took as her lover Aegisthus, the only surviving son of Thyestes. Agamemnon and Clytaemestra arranged a series of beacons between Argos and Troy, by which he would signal the capture of the city.

It is at this point that *Agamemnon* begins. The action contained in the play itself consists of a short, simple series of events: the return of Agamemnon, his formal reception and entrance into the palace, the murder of Agamemnon and Cassandra, and, at the end, the defiance of Argos and its citizens by Clytaemestra and Aegisthus. The power of the drama lies partly in the dramatic arrangements of these events, but also in the choral lyrics and long speeches, in which the tragic scenes of the past, flashbacks in memory, are made to enlarge and illuminate the action and persons before us: the departure for Troy, the portents, and the sacrifice of Iphigeneia; the relay of beacons to announce the fall of Troy; the fall of the city; the flight of Helen; the wreck of the fleet returning from Troy; and the murder of the children of Thyestes.

NOTE

The translation of *Agamemnon* that is here used first appeared in *Greek Plays in Modern Translation*, edited with an Introduction by Dudley Fitts (New York: Dial Press, 1947). It is used here by kind permission of The Dial Press, Inc. Some alterations have been made, chiefly in the matter of spelling Greek names. Two sections of *Agamemnon*, "The God of War, Money Changer of Dead Bodies," and "The Achaeans Have Got Troy, upon This Very Day," first published in *War and the Poet: A Comprehensive Anthology of the World's Great War Poetry*, edited by Richard Eberhart and Selden Rodman, are used by permission of The Devin-Adair Company.

The translation of this play is based on H. W. Smyth's "Loeb Classical Library" text (London and New York: William Heinemann, Ltd., and G. P. Putnam's Sons, 1926). A few deviations from this text occur where the translator has followed the manuscript readings instead of emendations accepted by Smyth.

Various editions of Greek drama divide the lines of lyric passages in various ways, but editors regularly follow the traditional line numbers whether their own line divisions tally with these numbers or not. This accounts for what may appear to be erratic line numbering in this translation. The line numbering in this translation is that of Smyth's text.

CHARACTERS

Watchman

Clytaemestra

Herald

Agamemnon

Cassandra

Aegisthus

Chorus of Argive Elders

Attendants of Clytaemestra: of Agamemnon: bodyguard of Aegisthus (all silent parts)

Time, directly after the fall of Troy.

AGAMEMNON

SCENE: *Argos, before the palace of King Agamemnon. The Watchman,*
who speaks the opening lines, is posted on the roof of the palace.
Clytaemestra's entrances are made from a door in the center of the
stage; all others, from the wings.

(The Watchman, alone.)

I ask the gods some respite from the weariness
of this watchtime measured by years I lie awake
elbowed upon the Atreidae's roof dogwise to mark
the grand processionals of all the stars of night
burdened with winter and again with heat for men,   5
dynasties in their shining blazoned on the air,
these stars, upon their wane and when the rest arise.

I wait; to read the meaning in that beacon light,
a blaze of fire to carry out of Troy the rumor
and outcry of its capture; to such end a lady's   10
male strength of heart in its high confidence ordains.
Now as this bed stricken with night and drenched with dew
I keep, nor ever with kind dreams for company:
since fear in sleep's place stands forever at my head
against strong closure of my eyes, or any rest: 15
I mince such medicine against sleep failed: I sing,
only to weep again the pity of this house
no longer, as once, administered in the grand way.
Now let there be again redemption from distress,
the flare burning from the blackness in good augury.   20

(A light shows in the distance.)

Oh hail, blaze of the darkness, harbinger of day's
shining, and of processionals and dance and choirs
of multitudes in Argos for this day of grace.
Ahoy!
I cry the news aloud to Agamemnon's queen,   25

that she may rise up from her bed of state with speed
to raise the rumor of gladness welcoming this beacon,
and singing rise, if truly the citadel of Ilium
has fallen, as the shining of this flare proclaims.
I also, I, will make my choral prelude, since   30
my lord's dice cast aright are counted as my own,
and mine the tripled sixes of this torchlit throw.

May it only happen. May my king come home, and I
take up within this hand the hand I love. The rest
I leave to silence; for an ox stands huge upon   35
my tongue. The house itself, could it take voice, might speak
aloud and plain. I speak to those who understand,
but if they fail, I have forgotten everything.

(*Exit. The Chorus enters, speaking.*)

Ten years since the great contestants   40
of Priam's right,
Menelaus and Agamemnon, my lord,
twin throned, twin sceptered, in twofold power
of kings from God, the Atreidae,
put forth from this shore   45
the thousand ships of the Argives,
the strength and the armies.
Their cry of war went shrill from the heart,
as eagles stricken in agony
for young perished, high from the nest   50
eddy and circle
to bend and sweep of the wings' stroke,
lost far below
the fledgelings, the nest, and the tendance.
Yet someone hears in the air, a god,   55
Apollo, Pan, or Zeus, the high
thin wail of these sky-guests, and drives
late to its mark
the Fury upon the transgressors.

So drives Zeus the great guest god   60

the Atreidae against Alexander:
for one woman's promiscuous sake
the struggling masses, legs tired,
knees grinding in dust,
spears broken in the onset.   65
Danaans and Trojans
they have it alike. It goes as it goes
now. The end will be destiny.
You cannot burn flesh or pour unguents,
not innocent cool tears,   70
that will soften the gods' stiff anger.

But we; dishonored, old in our bones,
cast off even then from the gathering horde,
stay here, to prop up
on staves the strength of a baby.   75
Since the young vigor that urges
inward to the heart
is frail as age, no warcraft yet perfect,
while beyond age, leaf
withered, man goes three footed   80
no stronger than a child is,
a dream that falters in daylight.

(Clytaemestra enters quietly. The Chorus continues to speak.)

But you, lady,
daughter of Tyndareus, Clytaemestra, our queen:
What is there to be done? What new thing have you heard?   85
In persuasion of what
report do you order such sacrifice?
To all the gods of the city,
the high and the deep spirits,
to them of the sky and the market places,   90
the altars blaze with oblations.
The staggered flame goes sky high
one place, then another,
drugged by the simple soft

persuasion of sacred unguents,   95
the deep stored oil of the kings.
Of these things what can be told
openly, speak.
Be healer to this perplexity
that grows now into darkness of thought,   100
while again sweet hope shining from the flames
beats back the pitiless pondering
of sorrow that eats my heart.

I have mastery yet to chant the wonder at the wayside
given to kings. Still by God's grace there surges within me   105
singing magic
grown to my life and power,
how the wild bird portent
hurled forth the Achaeans'
twin-stemmed power single hearted,   110
lords of the youth of Hellas,
with spear and hand of strength
to the land of Teucrus.
Kings of birds to the kings of the ships,
one black, one blazed with silver,   115
clear seen by the royal house
on the right, the spear hand,
they lighted, watched by all
tore a hare, ripe, bursting with young unborn yet,
stayed from her last fleet running.   120
Sing sorrow, sorrow: but good win out in the end.

Then the grave seer of the host saw through to the hearts divided,
knew the fighting sons of Atreus feeding on the hare
with the host, their people.
Seeing beyond, he spoke: 125
"With time, this foray
shall stalk the castle of Priam.
Before then, under
the walls, Fate shall spoil

in violence the rich herds of the people.   130
Only let no doom of the gods darken
upon this huge iron forged to curb Troy—
from inward. Artemis the undefiled
is angered with pity
at the flying hounds of her father   135
eating the unborn young in the hare and the shivering mother.
She is sick at the eagles' feasting.
Sing sorrow, sorrow: but good win out in the end.

Lovely you are and kind   140
to the tender young of ravening lions.
For sucklings of all the savage
beasts that lurk in the lonely places you have sympathy.
Grant meaning to these appearances
good, yet not without evil.   145
Healer Apollo, I pray you
let her not with cross winds
bind the ships of the Danaans
to time-long anchorage   150
forcing a second sacrifice unholy, untasted,
working bitterness in the blood
and faith lost. For the terror returns like sickness to lurk in the
      house;
the secret anger remembers the child that shall be avenged." 155
Such, with great good things beside, rang out in the voice of
      Calchas,
these fatal signs from the birds by the way to the house of the
      princes,
wherewith in sympathy
sing sorrow, sorrow: but good win out in the end.

Zeus: whatever he may be, if this name   160
pleases him in invocation,
thus I call upon him.
I have pondered everything
yet I cannot find a way,

only Zeus, to cast this dead weight of ignorance   165
finally from out my brain.

He who in time long ago was great,
throbbing with gigantic strength,
shall be as if he never were, unspoken.   170
He who followed him has found
his master, and is gone.
Cry aloud without fear the victory of Zeus,
you will not have failed the truth: 175

Zeus, who guided men to think,
who has laid it down that wisdom
comes alone through suffering.
Still there drips in sleep against the heart
grief of memory; against   180
our pleasure we are temperate.
From the gods who sit in grandeur
grace comes somehow violent.

On that day the elder king
of the Achaean ships, no more
strict against the prophet's word,   185
turned with the crosswinds of fortune,
when no ship sailed, no pail was full,
and the Achaean people sulked
fast against the shore at Aulis
facing Chalcis, where the tides ebb and surge: 190

and winds blew from the Strymon, bearing
sick idleness, ships tied fast, and hunger,
distraction of the mind, carelessness
for hull and cable;   195
with time's length bent to double measure
by delay crumbled the flower and pride
of Argos. Then against the bitter wind
the seer's voice clashed out
another medicine   200

more hateful yet, and spoke of Artemis, so that the kings
dashed their staves to the ground and could not hold their tears.

The elder lord spoke aloud before them: 205
"My fate is angry if I disobey these,
but angry if I slaughter
this child, the beauty of my house,
with maiden blood shed staining
these father's hands beside the altar.   210
What of these things goes now without disaster?
How shall I fail my ships
and lose my faith of battle?
For them to urge such sacrifice of innocent blood   215
angrily, for their wrath is great—it is right. May all be well yet."

But when necessity's yoke was put upon him
he changed, and from the heart the breath came bitter
and sacrilegious, utterly infidel,   220
to warp a will now to be stopped at nothing.
The sickening in men's minds, tough,
reckless in fresh cruelty brings daring. He endured then
to sacrifice his daughter
to stay the strength of war waged for a woman,   225
first offering for the ships' sake.

Her supplications and her cries of father
were nothing, nor the child's lamentation
to kings passioned for battle.   230
The father prayed, called to his men to lift her
with strength of hand swept in her robes aloft
and prone above the altar, as you might lift
a goat for sacrifice, with guards
against the lips' sweet edge, to check   235
the curse cried on the house of Atreus
by force of bit and speech drowned in strength.

Pouring then to the ground her saffron mantle
she struck the sacrificers with   240
the eyes' arrows of pity,

lovely as in a painted scene, and striving
to speak—as many times
at the kind festive table of her father
she had sung, and in the clear voice of a stainless maiden   245
with love had graced the song
of worship when the third cup was poured.

What happened next I saw not, neither speak it.
The crafts of Calchas fail not of outcome.
Justice so moves that those only learn   250
who suffer; and the future
you shall know when it has come; before then, forget it.
It is grief too soon given.
All will come clear in the next dawn's sunlight.
Let good fortune follow these things as   255
she who is here desires,
our Apian land's singlehearted protectress.

(The Chorus now turns toward Clytaemestra, and the leader
speaks to her.)

I have come in reverence, Clytaemestra, of your power.
For when the man is gone and the throne void, his right
falls to the prince's lady, and honor must be given.   260
Is it some grace—or otherwise—that you have heard
to make you sacrifice at messages of good hope?
I should be glad to hear, but must not blame your silence.

Clytaemestra

As it was said of old, may the dawn child be born
to be an angel of blessing from the kindly night.   265
You shall know joy beyond all you ever hoped to hear.
The men of Argos have taken Priam's citadel.

Chorus

What have you said? Your words escaped my unbelief.

Clytaemestra

The Achaeans are in Troy. Is that not clear enough?

Chorus

This slow delight steals over me to bring forth tears. 270

Clytaemestra

Yes, for your eyes betray the loyal heart within.

Chorus

Yet how can I be certain? Is there some evidence?

Clytaemestra

There is, there must be; unless a god has lied to me.

Chorus

Is it dream visions, easy to believe, you credit?

Clytaemestra

I accept nothing from a brain that is dull with sleep. 275

Chorus

The charm, then, of some rumor, that made rich your hope?

Clytaemestra

Am I some young girl, that you find my thoughts so silly?

Chorus

How long, then, is it since the citadel was stormed?

Clytaemestra

It is the night, the mother of this dawn I hailed.

Chorus

What kind of messenger could come in speed like this? 280

Clytaemestra

Hephaestus, who cast forth the shining blaze from Ida.
And beacon after beacon picking up the flare
carried it here; Ida to the Hermaean horn
of Lemnos, where it shone above the isle, and next
the sheer rock face of Zeus on Athos caught it up; 285
and plunging skyward to arch the shoulders of the sea
the strength of the running flare in exultation,
pine timbers flaming into gold, like the sunrise,

brought the bright message to Macistus' sentinel cliffs,
who, never slow nor in the carelessness of sleep   290
caught up, sent on his relay in the courier chain,
and far across Euripus' streams the beacon flare
carried to signal watchmen on Messapion.
These took it again in turn, and heaping high a pile
of silvery brush flamed it to throw the message on.   295
And the flare sickened never, but grown stronger yet
outleapt the river valley of Asopus like
the very moon for shining, to Cithaeron's scaur
to waken the next station of the flaming post.
These watchers, not contemptuous of the far-thrown blaze, 300
kindled another beacon vaster than commanded.
The light leaned high above Gorgopis' staring marsh,
and striking Aegyplanctus' mountain top, drove on
yet one more relay, lest the flare die down in speed.
Kindled once more with stintless heaping force, they send 305
the beard of flame to hugeness, passing far beyond
the promontory that gazes on the Saronic strait
and flaming far, until it plunged at last to strike
the steep rock of Arachnus near at hand, our watchtower.
And thence there fell upon this house of Atreus' sons   310
the flare whose fathers mount to the Idaean beacon.
These are the changes on my torchlight messengers,
one from another running out the laps assigned.
The first and the last sprinters have the victory.
By such proof and such symbol I announce to you   315
my lord at Troy has sent his messengers to me.

Chorus

The gods, lady, shall have my prayers and thanks straightway.
And yet to hear your story till all wonder fades
would be my wish, could you but tell it once again.

Clytaemestra

The Achaeans have got Troy, upon this very day.   320
I think the city echoes with a clash of cries.

Pour vinegar and oil into the selfsame bowl,
you could not say they mix in friendship, but fight on.
Thus variant sound the voices of the conquerors
and conquered, from the opposition of their fates. 325
Trojans are stooping now to gather in their arms
their dead, husbands and brothers; children lean to clasp
the aged who begot them, crying upon the death
of those most dear, from lips that never will be free.
The Achaeans have their midnight work after the fighting 330
that sets them down to feed on all the city has,
ravenous, headlong, by no rank and file assigned,
but as each man has drawn his shaken lot by chance.
And in the Trojan houses that their spears have taken
they settle now, free of the open sky, the frosts 335
and dampness of the evening; without sentinels set
they sleep the sleep of happiness the whole night through.
And if they reverence the gods who hold the city
and all the holy temples of the captured land,
they, the despoilers, might not be despoiled in turn. 340
Let not their passion overwhelm them; let no lust
seize on these men to violate what they must not.
The run to safety and home is yet to make; they must turn
the pole, and run the backstretch of the double course.
Yet, though the host come home without offence to high 345
gods, even so the anger of these slaughtered men
may never sleep. Oh, let there be no fresh wrong done!

Such are the thoughts you hear from me, a woman merely.
Yet may the best win through, that none may fail to see.
Of all good things to wish this is my dearest choice. 350

Chorus

My lady, no grave man could speak with better grace.
I have listened to the proofs of your tale, and I believe,
and go to make my glad thanksgivings to the gods.
This pleasure is not unworthy of the grief that gave it.

O Zeus our lord and Night beloved,   355
bestower of power and beauty,
you slung above the bastions of Troy
the binding net, that none, neither great
nor young, might outleap
the gigantic toils   360
of enslavement and final disaster.
I gaze in awe on Zeus of the guests
who wrung from Alexander such payment.
He bent the bow with slow care, that neither
the shaft might hurdle the stars, nor fall   365
spent to the earth, short driven.

They have the stroke of Zeus to tell of.
This thing is clear and you may trace it.
He acted as he had decreed. A man thought
the gods deigned not to punish mortals   370
who trampled down the delicacy of things
inviolable. That man was wicked.
The curse on great daring
shines clear; it wrings atonement   375
from those high hearts that drive to evil,
from houses blossoming to pride
and peril. Let there be
wealth without tears; enough for
the wise man who will ask no further.   380
There is not any armor
in gold against perdition
for him who spurns the high altar
of Justice down to the darkness.

Persuasion the persistent overwhelms him,   385
she, strong daughter of designing Ruin.
And every medicine is vain; the sin
smolders not, but burns to evil beauty.
As cheap bronze tortured   390
at the touchstone relapses

to blackness and grime, so this man
tested shows vain
as a child that strives to catch the bird flying
and wins shame that shall bring down his city.　　395
No god will hear such a man's entreaty,
but whoso turns to these ways
they strike him down in his wickedness.
This was Paris: he came
to the house of the sons of Atreus,　　400
stole the woman away, and shamed
the guest's right of the board shared.

She left among her people the stir and clamor
of shields and of spearheads,
the ships to sail and the armor.　　405
She took to Ilium her dowry, death.
She stepped forth lightly between the gates
daring beyond all daring. And the prophets
about the great house wept aloud and spoke:
"Alas, alas for the house and for the champions,　　410
alas for the bed signed with their love together.
Here now is silence, scorned, unreproachful.
The agony of his loss is clear before us.
Longing for her who lies beyond the sea
he shall see a phantom queen in his household.　　415
Her images in their beauty
are bitterness to her lord now
where in the emptiness of eyes
all passion has faded."

Shining in dreams the sorrowful　　420
memories pass; they bring him
vain delight only.
It is vain, to dream and to see splendors,
and the image slipping from the arms' embrace
escapes, not to return again,　　425
on wings drifting down the ways of sleep.

Such have the sorrows been in the house by the hearthside;
such have there been, and yet there are worse than these.
In all Hellas, for those who swarmed to the host
the heartbreaking misery   430
shows in the house of each.
Many are they who are touched at the heart by these things.
Those they sent forth they knew;
now, in place of the young men
urns and ashes are carried home   435
to the houses of the fighters.

The god of war, money changer of dead bodies,
held the balance of his spear in the fighting,
and from the corpse-fires at Ilium   440
sent to their dearest the dust
heavy and bitter with tears shed
packing smooth the urns with
ashes that once were men.
They praise them through their tears, how this man   445
knew well the craft of battle, how another
went down splendid in the slaughter:
and all for some strange woman.
Thus they mutter in secrecy,
and the slow anger creeps below their grief   450
at Atreus' sons and their quarrels.
There by the walls of Ilium
the young men in their beauty keep
graves deep in the alien soil
they hated and they conquered.   455

The citizens speak: their voice is dull with hatred.
The curse of the people must be paid for.
There lurks for me in the hooded night
terror of what may be told me.   460
The gods fail not to mark
those who have killed many.
The black Furies stalking the man

fortunate beyond all right
wrench back again the set of his life   465
and drop him to darkness. There among
the ciphers there is no more comfort
in power. And the vaunt of high glory
is bitterness; for God's thunderbolts
crash on the towering mountains.   470
Let me attain no envied wealth,
let me not plunder cities,
neither be taken in turn, and face
life in the power of another.

    (*Various members of the Chorus, speaking severally.*)

From the beacon's bright message   475
the fleet rumor runs
through the city. If this be real
who knows? Perhaps the gods have sent some lie to us.

Who of us is so childish or so reft of wit
that by the beacon's messages   480
his heart flamed must despond again
when the tale changes in the end?

It is like a woman indeed
to take the rapture before the fact has shown for true.

They believe too easily, are too quick to shift   485
from ground to ground; and swift indeed
the rumor voiced by a woman dies again.

Now we shall understand these torches and their shining,
the beacons, and the interchange of flame and flame.
They may be real; yet bright and dreamwise ecstasy   490
in light's appearance might have charmed our hearts awry.
I see a herald coming from the beach, his brows
shaded with sprigs of olive; and upon his feet
the dust, dry sister of the mire, makes plain to me   495
that he will find a voice, not merely kindle flame
from mountain timber, and make signals from the smoke,

but tell us outright, whether to be happy, or—
but I shrink back from naming the alternative.
That which appeared was good; may yet more good be given.   500

And any man who prays that different things befall
the city, may he reap the crime of his own heart.

(The Herald enters, and speaks.)

Soil of my fathers, Argive earth I tread upon,
in daylight of the tenth year I have come back to you.
All my hopes broke but one, and this I have at last.   505
I never could have dared to dream that I might die
in Argos, and be buried in this beloved soil.
Hail to the Argive land and to its sunlight, hail
to its high sovereign, Zeus, and to the Pythian king.
May you no longer shower your arrows on our heads.   510
Beside Scamandrus you were grim; be satisfied
and turn to savior now and healer of our hurts,
my lord Apollo. Gods of the market place assembled,
I greet you all, and my own patron deity
Hermes, beloved herald, in whose right all heralds   515
are sacred; and you heroes that sent forth the host,
propitiously take back all that the spear has left.
O great hall of the kings and house beloved; seats
of sanctity; divinities that face the sun:
if ever before, look now with kind and glowing eyes   520
to greet our king in state after so long a time.
He comes, lord Agamemnon, bearing light in gloom
to you, and to all that are assembled here.
Salute him with good favor, as he well deserves,
the man who has wrecked Ilium with the spade of Zeus   525
vindictive, whereby all their plain has been laid waste.
Gone are their altars, the sacred places of the gods
are gone, and scattered all the seed within the ground.
With such a yoke as this gripped to the neck of Troy
he comes, the king, Atreus' elder son, a man   530

fortunate to be honored far above all men
alive; not Paris nor the city tied to him
can boast he did more than was done him in return.
Guilty of rape and theft, condemned, he lost the prize
captured, and broke to sheer destruction all the house   535
of his fathers, with the very ground whereon it stood.
Twice over the sons of Priam have atoned their sins.

Chorus

Hail and be glad, herald of the Achaean host.

Herald

I am happy; I no longer ask the gods for death.

Chorus

Did passion for your country so strip bare your heart?   540

Herald

So that the tears broke in my eyes, for happiness.

Chorus

You were taken with that sickness, then, that brings delight.

Herald

How? I cannot deal with such words until I understand.

Chorus

Struck with desire of those who loved as much again.

Herald

You mean our country longed for us, as we for home?   545

Chorus

So that I sighed, out of the darkness of my heart.

Herald

Whence came this black thought to afflict the mind with fear?

Chorus

Long since it was my silence kept disaster off.

Herald

But how? There were some you feared when the kings went
    away?

Chorus

So much that as you said now, even death were grace.   550

Herald

Well: the end has been good. And in the length of time
part of our fortune you could say held favorable,
but part we cursed again. And who, except the gods,
can live time through forever without any pain?
Were I to tell you of the hard work done, the nights   555
exposed, the cramped sea-quarters, the foul beds—what part
of day's disposal did we not cry out loud?
Ashore, the horror stayed with us and grew. We lay
against the ramparts of our enemies, and from
the sky, and from the ground, the meadow dews came out   560
to soak our clothes and fill our hair with lice. And if
I were to tell of winter time, when all birds died,
the snows of Ida past endurance she sent down,
or summer heat, when in the lazy noon the sea
fell level and asleep under a windless sky—   565
but why live such grief over again? That time is gone
for us, and gone for those who died. Never again
need they rise up, nor care again for anything.
Why must a live man count the numbers of the slain,
why grieve at fortune's wrath that fades to break once more?   570
I call a long farewell to all our unhappiness.
For us, survivors of the Argive armament,
the pleasure wins, pain casts no weight in the opposite scale.
And here, in this sun's shining, we can boast aloud,
whose fame has gone with wings across the land and sea: 575
"Upon a time the Argive host took Troy, and on
the houses of the gods who live in Hellas nailed
the spoils, to be the glory of days long ago."
And they who hear such things shall call this city blest
and the leaders of the host; and high the grace of God   580
shall be exalted, that did this. You have the story.

Chorus

I must give way; your story shows that I was wrong.
Old men are always young enough to learn, with profit.

But Clytaemestra and her house must hear, above
others, this news that makes luxurious my life.   585

(*Clytaemestra comes forward and speaks.*)

I raised my cry of joy, and it was long ago
when the first beacon flare of message came by night
to speak of capture and of Ilium's overthrow.
But there was one who laughed at me, who said: "You trust   590
in beacons so, and you believe that Troy has fallen?
How like a woman, for the heart to lift so light."
Men spoke like that; they thought I wandered in my wits;
yet I made sacrifice, and in the womanish strain
voice after voice caught up the cry along the city   595
to echo in the temples of the gods and bless
and still the fragrant flame that melts the sacrifice.

Why should you tell me then the whole long tale at large
when from my lord himself I shall hear all the story?
But now, how best to speed my preparation to   600
receive my honored lord come home again—what else
is light more sweet for woman to behold than this,
to spread the gates before her husband home from war
and saved by God's hand?—take this message to the king:
Come, and with speed, back to the city that longs for him,   605
and may he find a wife within his house as true
as on the day he left her, watchdog of the house
gentle to him alone, fierce to his enemies,
and such a woman in all her ways as this, who has
not broken the seal upon her in the length of days.   610
With no man else have I known delight, nor any shame
of evil speech, more than I know how to temper bronze.

(*Clytaemestra goes to the back of the stage.*)

Herald

A vaunt like this, so loaded as it is with truth,
it well becomes a highborn lady to proclaim.

Chorus

    Thus has she spoken to you, and well you understand,   615
    words that impress interpreters whose thought is clear.
    But tell me, herald; I would learn of Menelaus,
    that power beloved in this land. Has he survived
    also, and come with you back to his home again?

Herald

    I know no way to lie and make my tale so fair   620
    that friends could reap joy of it for any length of time.

Chorus

    Is there no means to speak us fair, and yet tell the truth?
    It will not hide, when truth and good are torn asunder.

Herald

    He is gone out of the sight of the Achaean host,
    vessel and man alike. I speak no falsehood there.   625

Chorus

    Was it when he had put out from Ilium in your sight,
    or did a storm that struck you both whirl him away?

Herald

    How like a master bowman you have hit the mark
    and in your speech cut a long sorrow to brief stature.

Chorus

    But then the rumor in the host that sailed beside,   630
    was it that he had perished, or might yet be living?

Herald

    No man knows. There is none could tell us that for sure
    except the Sun, from whom this earth has life and increase.

Chorus

    How did this storm, by wrath of the divinities,
    strike on our multitude at sea? How did it end?   635

Herald

    It is not well to stain the blessing of this day
    with speech of evil weight. Such gods are honored apart.

And when the messenger of a shaken host, sad faced,
brings to his city news it prayed never to hear,
this scores one wound upon the body of the people;   640
and that from many houses many men are slain
by the two-lashed whip dear to the War God's hand, this turns
disaster double-bladed, bloodily made two.
The messenger so freighted with a charge of tears
should make his song of triumph at the Furies' door.   645
But, carrying the fair message of our hopes' salvation,
come home to a glad city's hospitality,
how shall I mix my gracious news with foul, and tell
of the storm on the Achaeans by God's anger sent?
For they, of old the deepest enemies, sea and fire,   650
made a conspiracy and gave the oath of hand
to blast in ruin our unhappy Argive army.
At night the sea began to rise in waves of death.
Ship against ship the Thracian stormwind shattered us,
and gored and split, our vessels, swept in violence   655
of storm and whirlwind, beaten by the breaking rain,
drove on in darkness, spun by the wicked shepherd's hand.
But when the sun came up again to light the dawn,
we saw the Aegaean Sea blossoming with dead men,
the men of Achaea, and the wreckage of their ships.   660
For us, and for our ship, some god, no man, by guile
or by entreaty's force prevailing, laid his hand
upon the helm and brought us through with hull unscarred.
Life-giving fortune deigned to take our ship in charge
that neither riding in deep water she took the surf   665
nor drove to shoal and break upon some rocky shore.
But then, delivered from death at sea, in the pale day,
incredulous of our own luck, we shepherded
in our sad thoughts the fresh disaster of the fleet
so pitifully torn and shaken by the storm.   670
Now of these others, if there are any left alive
they speak of us as men who perished, must they not?
Even as we, who fear that they are gone. But may

it all come well in the end. For Menelaus: be sure
if any of them come back that he will be the first.   675
If he is still where some sun's gleam can track him down,
alive and open-eyed, by blessed hand of God
who willed that not yet should his seed be utterly gone,
there is some hope that he will still come home again.
You have heard all; and be sure, you have heard the truth.   680

(The Herald goes out.)

Chorus

Who is he that named you so
fatally in every way?
Could it be some mind unseen
in divination of your destiny
shaping to the lips that name   685
for the bride of spears and blood,
Helen, which is death? Appropriately
death of ships, death of men and cities
from the bower's soft curtained   690
and secluded luxury she sailed then,
driven on the giant west wind,
and armored men in their thousands came,
huntsmen down the oar blade's fading footprint   695
to struggle in blood with those
who by the banks of Simoeis
beached their hulls where the leaves break.

And on Ilium in truth
in the likeness of the name   700
the sure purpose of the Wrath drove
marriage with death: for the guest board
shamed, and Zeus kindly to strangers,
the vengeance wrought on those men
who graced in too loud voice the bride-song   705
fallen to their lot to sing,
the kinsmen and the brothers.
And changing its song's measure

the ancient city of Priam   710
chants in high strain of lamentation,
calling Paris him of the fatal marriage;
for it endured its life's end
in desolation and tears
and the piteous blood of its people.   715

Once a man fostered in his house
a lion cub, from the mother's milk
torn, craving the breast given.
In the first steps of its young life   720
mild, it played with children
and delighted the old.
Caught in the arm's cradle
they pampered it like a newborn child,
shining eyed and broken to the hand   725
to stay the stress of its hunger.

But it grew with time, and the lion
in the blood strain came out; it paid
grace to those who had fostered it
in blood and death for the sheep flocks,   730
a grim feast forbidden.
The house reeked with blood run
nor could its people beat down the bane,
the giant murderer's onslaught.
This thing they raised in their house was blessed   735
by God to be priest of destruction.

And that which first came to the city of Ilium,
call it a dream of calm
and the wind dying,
the loveliness and luxury of much gold,   740
the melting shafts of the eyes' glances,
the blossom that breaks the heart with longing.
But she turned in mid-step of her course to make
bitter the consummation,   745

whirling on Priam's people
to blight with her touch and nearness.
Zeus hospitable sent her,
a vengeance to make brides weep.

It has been made long since and grown old among men,   750
this saying: human wealth
grown to fulness of stature
breeds again nor dies without issue.
From high good fortune in the blood   755
blossoms the quenchless agony.
Far from others I hold my own
mind; only the act of evil
breeds others to follow,
young sins in its own likeness.   760
Houses clear in their right are given
children in all loveliness.

But Pride aging is made
in men's dark actions
ripe with the young pride   765
late or soon when the dawn of destiny
comes and birth is given
to the spirit none may fight nor beat down,
sinful Daring; and in those halls
the black visaged Disasters stamped   770
in the likeness of their fathers.

And Righteousness is a shining in
the smoke of mean houses.
Her blessing is on the just man.   775
From high halls starred with gold by reeking hands
she turns back
with eyes that glance away to the simple in heart,
spurning the strength of gold
stamped false with flattery.   780
And all things she steers to fulfilment.

*(Agamemnon enters in a chariot, with Cassandra beside
him. The Chorus speaks to him.)*

Behold, my king: sacker of Troy's citadel,
own issue of Atreus.
How shall I hail you? How give honor   785
not crossing too high nor yet bending short
of this time's graces?
For many among men are they who set high
the show of honor, yet break justice.
If one be unhappy, all else are fain   790
to grieve with him: yet the teeth of sorrow
come nowise near to the heart's edge.
And in joy likewise they show joy's semblance,
and torture the face to the false smile.
Yet the good shepherd, who knows his flock,   795
the eyes of men cannot lie to him,
that with water of feigned
love seem to smile from the true heart.
But I: when you marshalled this armament
for Helen's sake, I will not hide it,   800
in ugly style you were written in my heart
for steering aslant the mind's course
to bring home by blood
sacrifice and dead men that wild spirit.
But now, in love drawn up from the deep heart,   805
not skimmed at the edge, we hail you.
You have won, your labor is made gladness.
Ask all men: you will learn in time
which of your citizens have been just
in the city's sway, which were reckless.   810

Agamemnon

To Argos first, and to the gods within the land,
I must give due greeting; they have worked with me to bring
me home; they helped me in the vengeance I have wrought
on Priam's city. Not from the lips of men the gods
heard justice, but in one firm cast they laid their votes   815

within the urn of blood that Ilium must die
and all her people; while above the opposite vase
the hand hovered and there was hope, but no vote fell.
The stormclouds of their ruin live; the ash that dies
upon them gushes still in smoke their pride of wealth. 820
For all this we must thank the gods with grace of much
high praise and memory, we who fenced within our toils
of wrath the city; and, because one woman strayed,
the beast of Argos broke them, the fierce young within
the horse, the armored people who marked out their leap 825
against the setting of the Pleiades. A wild
and bloody lion swarmed above the towers of Troy
to glut its hunger lapping at the blood of kings.

This to the gods, a prelude strung to length of words.
But, for the thought you spoke, I heard and I remember 830
and stand behind you. For I say that it is true.
In few men is it part of nature to respect
a friend's prosperity without begrudging him,
as envy's wicked poison settling to the heart
piles up the pain in one sick with unhappiness, 835
who, staggered under sufferings that are all his own,
winces again to the vision of a neighbor's bliss.
And I can speak, for I have seen, I know it well,
this mirror of companionship, this shadow's ghost,
these men who seemed my friends in all sincerity. 840
One man of them all, Odysseus, he who sailed unwilling,
once yoked to me carried his harness, nor went slack.
Dead though he be or living, I can say it still.

Now in the business of the city and the gods
we must ordain full conclave of all citizens 845
and take our counsel. We shall see what element
is strong, and plan that it shall keep its virtue still.
But that which must be healed—we must use medicine,
or burn, or amputate, with kind intention, take
all means at hand that might beat down corruption's pain. 850

So to the King's house and the home about the hearth
I take my way, with greeting to the gods within
who sent me forth, and who have brought me home once more.
My prize was conquest; may it never fail again.

(*Clytaemestra comes forward and speaks.*)

Grave gentlemen of Argolis assembled here,   855
I take no shame to speak aloud before you all
the love I bear my husband. In the lapse of time
modesty fades; it is human.

               What I tell you now
I learned not from another; this is my own sad life
all the long years this man was gone at Ilium.   860
It is evil and a thing of terror when a wife
sits in the house forlorn with no man by, and hears
rumors that like a fever die to break again,
and men come in with news of fear, and on their heels
another messenger, with worse news to cry aloud   865
here in this house. Had Agamemnon taken all
the wounds the tale whereof was carried home to me,
he had been cut full of gashes like a fishing net.
If he had died each time that rumor told his death,
he must have been some triple-bodied Geryon   870
back from the dead with threefold cloak of earth upon
his body, and killed once for every shape assumed.
Because such tales broke out forever on my rest,
many a time they cut me down and freed my throat   875
from the noose overslung where I had caught it fast.
And therefore is your son, in whom my love and yours
are sealed and pledged, not here to stand with us today,
Orestes. It were right; yet do not be amazed.
Strophius of Phocis, comrade in arms and faithful friend   880
to you, is keeping him. He spoke to me of peril
on two counts; of your danger under Ilium,
and here, of revolution and the clamorous people
who might cast down the council—since it lies in men's

nature to trample on the fighter already down.   885
Such my excuse to you, and without subterfuge.

For me: the rippling springs that were my tears have dried
utterly up, nor left one drop within. I keep
the pain upon my eyes where late at night I wept
over the beacons long ago set for your sake,   890
untended left forever. In the midst of dreams
the whisper that a gnat's thin wings could winnow broke
my sleep apart. I thought I saw you suffer wounds
more than the time that slept with me could ever hold.

Now all my suffering is past, with griefless heart   895
I hail this man, the watchdog of the fold and hall;
the stay that keeps the ship alive; the post to grip
groundward the towering roof; a father's single child;
land seen by sailors after all their hope was gone;
splendor of daybreak shining from the night of storm;   900
the running spring a parched wayfarer strays upon.
Oh, it is sweet to escape from all necessity!

Such is my greeting to him, that he well deserves.
Let none bear malice; for the harm that went before
I took, and it was great.
                              Now, my beloved one,   905
step from your chariot; yet let not your foot, my lord,
sacker of Ilium, touch the earth. My maidens there!
Why this delay? Your task has been appointed you,
to strew the ground before his feet with tapestries.
Let there spring up into the house he never hoped   910
to see, where Justice leads him in, a crimson path.

In all things else, my heart's unsleeping care shall act
with the gods' aid to set aright what fate ordained.

> (*Clytaemestra's handmaidens spread a bright carpet*
> *between the chariot and the door.*)

Agamemnon
Daughter of Leda, you who kept my house for me,
there is one way your welcome matched my absence well.   915

You strained it to great length. Yet properly to praise
me thus belongs by right to other lips, not yours.
And all this—do not try in woman's ways to make
me delicate, nor, as if I were some Asiatic
bow down to earth and with wide mouth cry out to me,   920
nor cross my path with jealousy by strewing the ground
with robes. Such state becomes the gods, and none beside.
I am a mortal, a man; I cannot trample upon
these tinted splendors without fear thrown in my path.
I tell you, as a man, not god, to reverence me.   925
Discordant is the murmur at such treading down
of lovely things; while God's most lordly gift to man
is decency of mind. Call that man only blest
who has in sweet tranquillity brought his life to close.
If I could only act as such, my hope is good.   930

Clytaemestra

Yet tell me this one thing, and do not cross my will.

Agamemnon

My will is mine. I shall not make it soft for you.

Clytaemestra

It was in fear surely that you vowed this course to God.

Agamemnon

No man has spoken knowing better what he said.

Clytaemestra

If Priam had won as you have, what would he have done?   935

Agamemnon

I well believe he might have walked on tapestries.

Clytaemestra

Be not ashamed before the bitterness of men.

Agamemnon

The people murmur, and their voice is great in strength.

Clytaemestra

    Yet he who goes unenvied shall not be admired.

Agamemnon

    Surely this lust for conflict is not womanlike?   940

Clytaemestra

    Yet for the mighty even to give way is grace.

Agamemnon

    Does such a victory as this mean so much to you?

Clytaemestra

    Oh yield! The power is yours. Give way of your free will.

Agamemnon

    Since you must have it—here, let someone with all speed
take off these sandals, slaves for my feet to tread upon.   945
And as I crush these garments stained from the rich sea
let no god's eyes of hatred strike me from afar.
Great the extravagance, and great the shame I feel
to spoil such treasure and such silver's worth of webs.

    So much for all this. Take this stranger girl within   950
now, and be kind. The conqueror who uses softly
his power, is watched from far in the kind eyes of God,
and this slave's yoke is one no man will wear from choice.
Gift of the host to me, and flower exquisite
from all my many treasures, she attends me here.   955

    Now since my will was bent to listen to you in this
my feet crush purple as I pass within the hall.

Clytaemestra

    The sea is there, and who shall drain its yield? It breeds
precious as silver, ever of itself renewed,
the purple ooze wherein our garments shall be dipped.   960
And by God's grace this house keeps full sufficiency
of all. Poverty is a thing beyond its thought.
I could have vowed to trample many splendors down

had such decree been ordained from the oracles
those days when all my study was to bring home your life.   965
For when the root lives yet the leaves will come again
to fence the house with shade against the Dog Star's heat,
and now you have come home to keep your hearth and house
you bring with you the symbol of our winter's warmth;
but when Zeus ripens the green clusters into wine   970
there shall be coolness in the house upon those days
because the master ranges his own halls once more.

Zeus, Zeus accomplisher, accomplish these my prayers.
Let your mind bring these things to pass. It is your will.

(*Agamemnon and Clytaemestra enter the house. Cassandra
remains in the chariot. The Chorus speaks.*)

Why must this persistent fear   975
beat its wings so ceaselessly
and so close against my mantic heart?
Why this strain unwanted, unrepaid, thus prophetic?
Nor can valor of good hope   980
seated near the chambered depth
of the spirit cast it out
as dreams of dark fancy; and yet time
has buried in the mounding sand
the sea cables since that day   985
when against Ilium
the army and the ships put to sea.

Yet I have seen with these eyes
Agamemnon home again.
Still the spirit sings, drawing deep   990
from within this unlyric threnody of the Fury.
Hope is gone utterly,
the sweet strength is far away.
Surely this is not fantasy.   995
Surely it is real, this whirl of drifts
that spin the stricken heart.
Still I pray; may all this

expectation fade as vanity
into unfulfilment, and not be.   1000

Yet it is true: the high strength of men
knows no content with limitation. Sickness
chambered beside it beats at the wall between.
Man's fate that sets a true   1005
course yet may strike upon
the blind and sudden reefs of disaster.
But if before such time, fear
throw overboard some precious thing
of the cargo, with deliberate cast,   1010
not all the house, laboring
with weight of ruin, shall go down,
nor sink the hull deep within the sea.
And great and affluent the gift of Zeus
in yield of ploughed acres year on year   1015
makes void again sick starvation.

But when the black and mortal blood of man
has fallen to the ground before his feet, who then   1020
can sing spells to call it back again?
Did Zeus not warn us once
when he struck to impotence
that one who could in truth charm back the dead men?
Had the gods not so ordained   1025
that fate should stand against fate
to check any man's excess,
my heart now would have outrun speech
to break forth the water of its grief.
But this is so; I murmur deep in darkness   1030
sore at heart; my hope is gone now
ever again to unwind some crucial good
from the flames about my heart.

                    (*Clytaemestra comes out from the house again*
                              and speaks to Cassandra.)

Cassandra, you may go within the house as well,   1035
since Zeus in no unkindness has ordained that you

must share our lustral water, stand with the great throng
of slaves that flock to the altar of our household god.
Step from this chariot, then, and do not be so proud.
And think—they say that long ago Alcmena's son   1040
was sold in bondage and endured the bread of slaves.
But if constraint of fact forces you to such fate,
be glad indeed for masters ancient in their wealth.
They who have reaped success beyond their dreams of hope
are savage above need and standard toward their slaves.   1045
From us you shall have all you have the right to ask.

Chorus

What she has spoken is for you, and clear enough.
Fenced in these fatal nets wherein you find yourself
you should obey her if you can; perhaps you can not.

Clytaemestra

Unless she uses speech incomprehensible,   1050
barbarian, wild as the swallow's song, I speak
within her understanding, and she must obey.

Chorus

Go with her. What she bids is best in circumstance
that rings you now. Obey, and leave this carriage seat.

Clytaemestra

I have no leisure to stand outside the house and waste   1055
time on this woman. At the central altarstone
the flocks are standing, ready for the sacrifice
we make to this glad day we never hoped to see.
You: if you are obeying my commands at all, be quick.
But if in ignorance you fail to comprehend,   1060
speak not, but make with your barbarian hand some sign.

Chorus

I think this stranger girl needs some interpreter
who understands. She is like some captive animal.

Clytaemestra

No, she is in the passion of her own wild thoughts.
Leaving her captured city she has come to us   1065

untrained to take the curb, and will not understand
until her rage and strength have foamed away in blood.
I shall throw down no more commands for her contempt.

(*Clytaemestra goes back into the house.*)

Chorus

I, though, shall not be angry, for I pity her.
Come down, poor creature, leave the empty car. Give way   1070
to compulsion and take up the yoke that shall be yours.

(*Cassandra descends from the chariot and cries out loud.*)

Oh shame upon the earth!
Apollo, Apollo!

Chorus

You cry on Loxias in agony? He is not
of those immortals the unhappy supplicate.   1075

Cassandra

Oh shame upon the earth!
Apollo, Apollo!

Chorus

Now once again in bitter voice she calls upon
this god, who has not part in any lamentation.

Cassandra

Apollo, Apollo!   1080
Lord of the ways, my ruin.
You have undone me once again, and utterly.

Chorus

I think she will be prophetic of her own disaster.
Even in the slave's heart the gift divine lives on.

Cassandra

Apollo, Apollo!   1085
Lord of the ways, my ruin.
Where have you led me now at last? What house is this?

Chorus

    The house of the Atreidae. If you understand
    not that, I can tell you; and so much at least is true.

Cassandra

    No, but a house that God hates, guilty within   1090
    of kindred blood shed, torture of its own,
    the shambles for men's butchery, the dripping floor.

Chorus

    The stranger is keen scented like some hound upon
    the trail of blood that leads her to discovered death.

Cassandra

    Behold there the witnesses to my faith.   1095
    The small children wail for their own death
    and the flesh roasted that their father fed upon.

Chorus

    We had been told before of this prophetic fame
    of yours: we want no prophets in this place at all.

Cassandra

    Ah, for shame, what can she purpose now?   1100
    What is this new and huge
    stroke of atrocity she plans within the house
    to beat down the beloved beyond hope of healing?
    Rescue is far away.

Chorus

    I can make nothing of these prophecies. The rest   1105
    I understood; the city is full of the sound of them.

Cassandra

    So cruel then, that you can do this thing?
    The husband of your own bed
    to bathe bright with water—how shall I speak the end?
    This thing shall be done with speed. The hand gropes now, and
        the other   1110
    hand follows in turn.

Chorus

    No, I am lost. After the darkness of her speech
    I go bewildered in a mist of prophecies.

Cassandra

    No, no, see there! What is that thing that shows?
    Is it some net of death?   1115
    Or is the trap the woman there, the murderess?
    Let now the slakeless fury in the race
    rear up to howl aloud over this monstrous death.

Chorus

    Upon what demon in the house do you call, to raise
    the cry of triumph? All your speech makes dark my hope.   1120
    And to the heart below trickles the pale drop
    as in the hour of death
    timed to our sunset and the mortal radiance.
    Ruin is near, and swift.

Cassandra

    See there, see there! Keep from his mate the bull.   1125
    Caught in the folded web's
    entanglement she pinions him and with the black horn
    strikes. And he crumples in the watered bath.
    Guile, I tell you, and death there in the caldron wrought.

Chorus

    I am not proud in skill to guess at prophecies,   1130
    yet even I can see the evil in this thing.
    From divination what good ever has come to men?
    Art, and multiplication of words
    drifting through tangled evil bring
    terror to them that hear.   1135

Cassandra

    Alas, alas for the wretchedness of my ill-starred life.
    This pain flooding the song of sorrow is mine alone.
    Why have you brought me here in all unhappiness?
    Why, why? Except to die with him? What else could be?

Chorus

> You are possessed of God, mazed at heart   1140
> to sing your own death
> song, the wild lyric as
> in clamor for Itys, Itys over and over again
> her long life of tears weeping forever grieves
> the brown nightingale.   1145

Cassandra

> Oh for the nightingale's pure song and a fate like hers.
> With fashion of beating wings the gods clothed her about
> and a sweet life gave her and without lamentation.
> But mine is the sheer edge of the tearing iron.

Chorus

> Whence come, beat upon beat, driven of God,   1150
> vain passions of tears?
> Whence your cries, terrified, clashing in horror,
> in wrought melody and the singing speech?
> Whence take you the marks to this path of prophecy
> and speech of terror?   1155

Cassandra

> Oh marriage of Paris, death to the men beloved!
> Alas, Scamandrus, water my fathers drank.
> There was a time I too at your springs
> drank and grew strong. Ah me,
> for now beside the deadly rivers, Cocytus   1160
> and Acheron, I must cry out my prophecies.

Chorus

> What is this word, too clear, you have uttered now?
> A child could understand.
> And deep within goes the stroke of the dripping fang
> as mortal pain at the trebled song of your agony   1165
> shivers the heart to hear.

Cassandra

> O sorrow, sorrow of my city dragged to uttermost death.
> O sacrifices my father made at the wall.

Flocks of the pastured sheep slaughtered there.
And no use at all   1170
to save our city from its pain inflicted now.
And I too, with brain ablaze in fever, shall go down.

Chorus

This follows the run of your song.
Is it, in cruel force of weight,
some divinity kneeling upon you brings   1175
the death song of your passionate suffering?
I can not see the end.

Cassandra

No longer shall my prophecies like some young girl
new-married glance from under veils, but bright and strong
as winds blow into morning and the sun's uprise   1180
shall wax along the swell like some great wave, to burst
at last upon the shining of this agony.
Now I will tell you plainly and from no cryptic speech;
bear me then witness, running at my heels upon
the scent of these old brutal things done long ago.   1185
There is a choir that sings as one, that shall not again
leave this house ever; the song thereof breaks harsh with menace.
And drugged to double fury on the wine of men's
blood shed, there lurks forever here a drunken rout
of ingrown vengeful spirits never to be cast forth.   1190
Hanging above the hall they chant their song of hate
and the old sin; and taking up the strain in turn
spit curses on that man who spoiled his brother's bed.
Did I go wide, or hit, like a real archer? Am I
some swindling seer who hawks his lies from door to door?   1195
Upon your oath, bear witness that I know by heart
the legend of ancient wickedness within this house.

Chorus

And how could an oath, though cast in rigid honesty,
do any good? And still we stand amazed at you,

reared in an alien city far beyond the sea,   1200
how can you strike, as if you had been there, the truth.

Cassandra

Apollo was the seer who set me to this work.

Chorus

Struck with some passion for you, and himself a god?

Cassandra

There was a time I blushed to speak about these things.

Chorus

True; they who prosper take on airs of vanity.   1205

Cassandra

Yes, then; he wrestled with me, and he breathed delight.

Chorus

Did you come to the getting of children then, as people do?

Cassandra

I promised that to Loxias, but I broke my word.

Chorus

Were you already ecstatic in the skills of God?

Cassandra

Yes; even then I read my city's destinies.   1210

Chorus

So Loxias' wrath did you no harm? How could that be?

Cassandra

For this my trespass, none believed me ever again.

Chorus

But we do; all that you foretell seems true to us.

Cassandra

But this is evil, see!
Now once again the pain of grim, true prophecy   1215
shivers my whirling brain in a storm of things foreseen.

Look there, see what is hovering above the house,
so small and young, imaged as in the shadow of dreams,
like children almost, killed by those most dear to them,
and their hands filled with their own flesh, as food to eat.   1220
I see them holding out the inward parts, the vitals,
oh pitiful, that meat their father tasted of. . . .
I tell you: There is one that plots vengeance for this,
the strengthless lion rolling in his master's bed,
who keeps, ah me, the house against his lord's return;   1225
my lord too, now that I wear the slave's yoke on my neck.
King of the ships, who tore up Ilium by the roots,
what does he know of this accursed bitch, who licks
his hand, who fawns on him with lifted ears, who like
a secret death shall strike the coward's stroke, nor fail?   1230
No, this is daring when the female shall strike down
the male. What can I call her and be right? What beast
of loathing? Viper double-fanged, or Scylla witch
holed in the rocks and bane of men that range the sea;
smoldering mother of death to smoke relentless hate   1235
on those most dear. How she stood up and howled aloud
and unashamed, as at the breaking point of battle,
in feigned gladness for his salvation from the sea!
What does it matter now if men believe or no?
What is to come will come. And soon you too will stand   1240
beside, to murmur in pity that my words were true.

Chorus

Thyestes' feast upon the flesh of his own children
I understand in terror at the thought, and fear
is on me hearing truth and no tale fabricated.
The rest: I heard it, but wander still far from the course.   1245

Cassandra

I tell you, you shall look on Agamemnon dead.

Chorus

Peace, peace, poor woman; put those bitter lips to sleep.

Cassandra

Useless; there is no god of healing in this story.

Chorus

Not if it must be; may it somehow fail to come.

Cassandra

Prayers, yes; they do not pray; they plan to strike, and kill.   1250

Chorus

What man is it who moves this beastly thing to be?

Cassandra

What man? You did mistake my divination then.

Chorus

It may be; I could not follow through the schemer's plan.

Cassandra

Yet I know Greek; I think I know it far too well.

Chorus

And Pythian oracles are Greek, yet hard to read.   1255

Cassandra

Oh, flame and pain that sweeps me once again! My lord,
Apollo, King of Light, the pain, aye me, the pain!
This is the woman-lioness, who goes to bed
with the wolf, when her proud lion ranges far away,
and she will cut me down; as a wife mixing drugs   1260
she wills to shred the virtue of my punishment
into her bowl of wrath as she makes sharp the blade
against her man, death that he brought a mistress home.
Why do I wear these mockeries upon my body,
this staff of prophecy, these flowers at my throat?   1265
At least I will spoil you before I die. Out, down,
break, damn you! This for all that you have done to me.
Make someone else, not me, luxurious in disaster. . . .
Lo now, this is Apollo who has stripped me here
of my prophetic robes. He watched me all the time   1270

« 45 »

wearing this glory, mocked of all, my dearest ones
who hated me with all their hearts, so vain, so wrong;
called like some gypsy wandering from door to door
beggar, corrupt, half-starved, and I endured it all.
And now the seer has done with me, his prophetess,   1275
and led me into such a place as this, to die.
Lost are my father's altars, but the block is there
to reek with sacrificial blood, my own. We two
must die, yet die not vengeless by the gods. For there
shall come one to avenge us also, born to slay   1280
his mother, and to wreak death for his father's blood.
Outlaw and wanderer, driven far from his own land,
he will come back to cope these stones of inward hate.
For this is a strong oath and sworn by the high gods,
that he shall cast men headlong for his father felled.   1285
Why am I then so pitiful? Why must I weep?
Since once I saw the citadel of Ilium
die as it died, and those who broke the city, doomed
by the gods, fare as they have fared accordingly,
I will go through with it. I too will take my fate.   1290
I call as on the gates of death upon these gates
to pray only for this thing, that the stroke be true,
and that with no convulsion, with a rush of blood
in painless death, I may close up these eyes, and rest.

Chorus

O woman much enduring and so greatly wise,   1295
you have said much. But if this thing you know be true,
this death that comes upon you, how can you, serene,
walk to the altar like a driven ox of God?

Cassandra

Friends, there is no escape for any longer time.

Chorus

Yet longest left in time is to be honored still.   1300

Cassandra

The day is here and now; I can not win by flight.

Chorus

Woman, be sure your heart is brave; you can take much.

Cassandra

None but the unhappy people ever hear such praise.

Chorus

Yet there is a grace on mortals who so nobly die.

Cassandra

Alas for you, father, and for your lordly sons.   1305
Ah!

Chorus

What now? What terror whirls you backward from the door?

Cassandra

Foul, foul!

Chorus

What foulness then, unless some horror in the mind?

Cassandra

That room within reeks with blood like a slaughter house.

Chorus

What then? Only these victims butchered at the hearth.   1310

Cassandra

There is a breath about it like an open grave.

Chorus

This is no Syrian pride of frankincense you mean.

Cassandra

So. I am going in, and mourning as I go
my death and Agamemnon's. Let my life be done.
Ah friends,   1315
truly this is no wild bird fluttering at a bush,
nor vain my speech. Bear witness to me when I die,
when falls for me, a woman slain, another woman,

and when a man dies for this wickedly mated man.
Here in my death I claim this stranger's grace of you.   1320

Chorus

Poor wretch, I pity you the fate you see so clear.

Cassandra

Yet once more will I speak, and not this time my own
death's threnody. I call upon the Sun in prayer
against that ultimate shining when the avengers strike
these monsters down in blood, that they avenge as well   1325
one simple slave who died, a small thing, lightly killed.

Alas, poor men, their destiny. When all goes well
a shadow will overthrow it. If it be unkind
one stroke of a wet sponge wipes all the picture out;
and that is far the most unhappy thing of all.   1330

(*Cassandra goes slowly into the house.*)

Chorus

High fortune is a thing slakeless
for mortals. There is no man who shall point
his finger to drive it back from the door
and speak the words: "Come no longer."
Now to this man the blessed ones have given   1335
Priam's city to be captured
and return in the gods' honor.
Must he give blood for generations gone,
die for those slain and in death pile up
more death to come for the blood shed,   1340
what mortal else who hears shall claim
he was born clear of the dark angel?

(*Agamemnon, inside the house.*)

Ah, I am struck a deadly blow and deep within!

Chorus

Silence: who cried out that he was stabbed to death within
   the house?

Agamemnon

Ah me, again, they struck again. I am wounded twice.   1345

Chorus

How the king cried out aloud to us! I believe the thing is done.
Come, let us put our heads together, try to find some safe way
out.

> (*The members of the Chorus go about distractedly,*
> *each one speaking in turn.*)

Listen, let me tell you what I think is best to do.
Let the herald call all citizens to rally here.

No, better to burst in upon them now, at once,   1350
and take them with the blood still running from their blades.

I am with this man and I cast my vote to him.
Act now. This is the perilous and instant time.

Anyone can see it, by these first steps they have taken,
they purpose to be tyrants here upon our city.   1355

Yes, for we waste time, while they trample to the ground
deliberation's honor, and their hands sleep not.

I can not tell which counsel of yours to call my own.
It is the man of action who can plan as well.

I feel as he does; nor can I see how by words   1360
we shall set the dead man back upon his feet again.

Do you mean, to drag our lives out long, that we must yield
to the house shamed, and leadership of such as these?

No, we can never endure that; better to be killed.
Death is a softer thing by far than tyranny.   1365

Shall we, by no more proof than that he cried in pain,
be sure, as by divination, that our lord is dead?

Yes, we should know what is true before we break our rage.
Here is sheer guessing and far different from sure knowledge.

From all sides the voices multiply to make me choose   1370
this course; to learn first how it stands with Agamemnon.

(*The doors of the palace open, disclosing the bodies of*
Agamemnon and Cassandra, with Clytaemestra
standing over them.)

Clytaemestra

Much have I said before to serve necessity,
but I will take no shame now to unsay it all.
How else could I, arming hate against hateful men
disguised in seeming tenderness, fence high the nets   1375
of ruin beyond overleaping? Thus to me
the conflict born of ancient bitterness is not
a thing new thought upon, but pondered deep in time.
I stand now where I struck him down. The thing is done.
Thus have I wrought, and I will not deny it now.   1380
That he might not escape nor beat aside his death,
as fishermen cast their huge circling nets, I spread
deadly abundance of rich robes, and caught him fast.
I struck him twice. In two great cries of agony
he buckled at the knees and fell. When he was down   1385
I struck him the third blow, in thanks and reverence
to Zeus the lord of dead men underneath the ground.
Thus he went down, and the life struggled out of him;
and as he died he spattered me with the dark red
and violent driven rain of bitter savored blood   1390
to make me glad, as gardens stand among the showers
of God in glory at the birthtime of the buds.

These being the facts, elders of Argos assembled here,
be glad, if it be your pleasure; but for me, I glory.
Were it religion to pour wine above the slain,   1395
this man deserved, more than deserved, such sacrament.
He filled our cup with evil things unspeakable
and now himself come home has drunk it to the dregs.

Chorus

We stand here stunned. How can you speak this way, with mouth
so arrogant, to vaunt above your fallen lord?   1400

Clytaemestra

> You try me out as if I were a woman and vain;
> but my heart is not fluttered as I speak before you.
> You know it. You can praise or blame me as you wish;
> it is all one to me. That man is Agamemnon,
> my husband; he is dead; the work of this right hand   1405
> that struck in strength of righteousness. And that is that.

Chorus

> Woman, what evil thing planted upon the earth
> or dragged from the running salt sea could you have tasted now
> to wear such brutality and walk in the people's hate?
> You have cast away, you have cut away. You shall go homeless
>   now,   1410
> crushed with men's bitterness.

Clytaemestra

> Now it is I you doom to be cast out from my city
> with men's hate heaped and curses roaring in my ears.
> Yet look upon this dead man; you would not cross him once
> when with no thought more than as if a beast had died,   1415
> when his ranged pastures swarmed with the deep fleece of flocks,
> he slaughtered like a victim his own child, my pain
> grown into love, to charm away the winds of Thrace.
> Were you not bound to hunt him then clear of this soil
> for the guilt stained upon him? Yet you hear what I   1420
> have done, and lo, you are a stern judge. But I say to you:
> go on and threaten me, but know that I am ready,
> if fairly you can beat me down beneath your hand,
> for you to rule; but if the god grant otherwise,
> you shall be taught—too late, for sure—to keep your place.   1425

Chorus

> Great your design, your speech is a clamor of pride.
> Swung to the red act drives the fury within your brain
> signed clear in the splash of blood over your eyes.
> Yet to come is stroke given for stroke
> vengeless, forlorn of friends.   1430

Clytaemestra

Now hear you this, the right behind my sacrament:
By my child's Justice driven to fulfilment, by
her Wrath and Fury, to whom I sacrificed this man,
the hope that walks my chambers is not traced with fear
while yet Aegisthus makes the fire shine on my hearth,   1435
my good friend, now as always, who shall be for us
the shield of our defiance, no weak thing; while he,
this other, is fallen, stained with this woman you behold,
plaything of all the golden girls at Ilium;
and here lies she, the captive of his spear, who saw   1440
wonders, who shared his bed, the wise in revelations
and loving mistress, who yet knew the feel as well
of the men's rowing benches. Their reward is not
unworthy. He lies there; and she who swanlike cried
aloud her lyric mortal lamentation out   1445
is laid against his fond heart, and to me has given
a delicate excitement to my bed's delight.

Chorus

O that in speed, without pain
and the slow bed of sickness
death could come to us now, death that forever   1450
carries sleep without ending, now that our lord is down,
our shield, kindest of men,
who for a woman's grace suffered so much,
struck down at last by a woman.

Alas, Helen, wild heart   1455
for the multitudes, for the thousand lives
you killed under Troy's shadow,
you alone, to shine in man's memory
as blood flower never to be washed out. Surely a demon then   1460
of death walked in the house, men's agony.

Clytaemestra

No, be not so heavy, nor yet draw down
in prayer death's ending,

neither turn all wrath against Helen
for men dead, that she alone killed 1465
all those Danaan lives, to work
the grief that is past all healing.

Chorus

Divinity that kneel on this house and the two
strains of the blood of Tantalus,
in the hands and hearts of women you steer 1470
the strength tearing my heart.
Standing above the corpse, obscene
as some carrion crow she sings
the crippled song and is proud.

Clytaemestra

Thus have you set the speech of your lips 1475
straight, calling by name
the spirit thrice glutted that lives in this race.
From him deep in the nerve is given
the love and the blood drunk, that before
the old wound dries, it bleeds again. 1480

Chorus

Surely it is a huge
and heavy spirit bending the house you cry;
alas, the bitter glory
of a doom that shall never be done with;
and all through Zeus, Zeus, 1485
first cause, prime mover.
For what thing without Zeus is done among mortals?
What here is without God's blessing?

O king, my king
how shall I weep for you?
What can I say out of my heart of pity? 1490
Caught in this spider's web you lie,
Your life gasped out in indecent death,
struck prone to this shameful bed

by your lady's hand of treachery   1495
and the stroke twin edged of the iron.

Clytaemestra

Can you claim I have done this?
Speak of me never
more as the wife of Agamemnon.
In the shadow of this corpse's queen   1500
the old stark avenger
of Atreus for his revel of hate
struck down this man,
last blood for the slaughtered children.

Chorus

What man shall testify   1505
your hands are clean of this murder?
How? How? Yet from his father's blood
might swarm some fiend to guide you.
The black ruin that shoulders
through the streaming blood of brothers   1510
strides at last where he shall win requital
for the children who were eaten.

O king, my king
how shall I weep for you?
What can I say out of my heart of pity?   1515
Caught in this spider's web you lie,
your life gasped out in indecent death,
struck prone to this shameful bed
by your lady's hand of treachery
and the stroke twin edged of the iron.   1520

Clytaemestra

No shame, I think, in the death given
this man. And did he not
first of all in this house wreak death
by treachery?
The flower of this man's love and mine,   1525

Iphigeneia of the tears
he dealt with even as he has suffered.
Let his speech in death's house be not loud.
With the sword he struck,
with the sword he paid for his own act.

Chorus

My thoughts are swept away and I go bewildered.   1530
Where shall I turn the brain's
activity in speed when the house is falling?
There is fear in the beat of the blood rain breaking
wall and tower. The drops come thicker.
Still fate grinds on yet more stones the blade   1535
for more acts of terror.

Earth, my earth, why did you not fold me under
before ever I saw this man lie dead
fenced by the tub in silver?   1540
Who shall bury him? Who shall mourn him?
Shall you dare this who have killed
your lord? Make lamentation,
render the graceless grace to his soul   1545
for huge things done in wickedness?
Who over this great man's grave shall lay
the blessing of tears
worked soberly from a true heart?   1550

Clytaemestra

Not for you to speak of such tendance.
Through us he fell,
by us he died; we shall bury.
There will be no tears in this house for him.
It must be Iphigeneia   1555
his child, who else,
shall greet her father by the whirling stream
and the ferry of tears
to close him in her arms and kiss him.

Chorus

Here is anger for anger. Between them
who shall judge lightly?
The spoiler is robbed; he killed, he has paid.
The truth stands ever beside God's throne
eternal: he who has wrought shall pay; that is law.
Then who shall tear the curse from their blood?
The seed is stiffened to ruin.

1560

1565

Clytaemestra

You see truth in the future
at last. Yet I wish
to seal my oath with the Spirit
in the house: I will endure all things as they stand
now, hard though it be. Hereafter
let him go forth to make bleed with death
and guilt the houses of others.
I will take some small
measure of our riches, and be content
that I swept from these halls
the murder, the sin, and the fury.

1570

1575

> (*Aegisthus enters, followed at a little distance by his
> armed bodyguard.*)

Aegisthus

O splendor and exaltation of this day of doom!
Now I can say once more that the high gods look down
on mortal crimes to vindicate the right at last,
now that I see this man—sweet sight—before me here
sprawled in the tangling nets of fury, to atone
the calculated evil of his father's hand.
For Atreus, this man's father, King of Argolis—
I tell you the clear story—drove my father forth,
Thyestes, his own brother, who had challenged him
in his king's right—forth from his city and his home.
Yet sad Thyestes came again to supplicate
the hearth, and win some grace, in that he was not slain

1580

1585

nor soiled the doorstone of his fathers with blood spilled.
Not his own blood. But Atreus, this man's godless sire,   1590
angrily hospitable set a feast for him,
in seeming a glad day of fresh meat slain and good
cheer; then served my father his own children's flesh
to feed on. For he carved away the extremities,
hands, feet, and cut the flesh apart, and covered them   1595
served in a dish to my father at his table apart,
who with no thought for the featureless meal before him ate
that ghastly food whose curse works now before your eyes.
But when he knew the terrible thing that he had done,
he spat the dead meat from him with a cry, and reeled   1600
spurning the table back to heel with strength the curse:
"Thus crash in ruin all the seed of Pleisthenes."
Out of such acts you see this dead man stricken here,
and it was I, in my right, who wrought this murder, I
third born to my unhappy father, and with him   1605
driven, a helpless baby in arms, to banishment.
Yet I grew up, and justice brought me home again,
till from afar I laid my hands upon this man,
since it was I who pieced together the fell plot.
Now I can die in honor again, if die I must,   1610
having seen him caught in the cords of his just punishment.

Chorus

Aegisthus, this strong vaunting in distress is vile,
You claim that you deliberately killed the king,
you, and you only, wrought the pity of this death.
I tell you then: There shall be no escape, your head   1615
shall face the stones of anger from the people's hands.

Aegisthus

So loud from you, stooped to the meanest rowing bench
with the ship's masters lordly on the deck above?
You are old men; well, you shall learn how hard it is
at your age, to be taught how to behave yourselves.   1620
But there are chains, there is starvation with its pain,

excellent teachers of good manners to old men,
wise surgeons and exemplars. Look! Can you not see it?
Lash not at the goads for fear you hit them, and be hurt.

Chorus

So then you, like a woman, waited the war out   1625
here in the house, shaming the master's bed with lust,
and planned against the lord of war this treacherous death?

Aegisthus

It is just such words as these will make you cry in pain.
Not yours the lips of Orpheus, no, quite otherwise,
whose voice of rapture dragged all creatures in his train.   1630
You shall be dragged, for baby whimperings sobbed out
in rage. Once broken, you will be easier to deal with.

Chorus

How shall you be lord of the men of Argos, you
who planned the murder of this man, yet could not dare
to act it out, and cut him down with your own hand?   1635

Aegisthus

No, clearly the deception was the woman's part,
and I was suspect, that had hated him so long.
Still with his money I shall endeavor to control
the citizens. The mutinous man shall feel the yoke
drag at his neck, no cornfed racing colt that runs   1640
free traced; but hunger, grim companion of the dark
dungeon shall see him broken to the hand at last.

Chorus

But why, why then, you coward, could you not have slain
your man yourself? Why must it be his wife who killed,
to curse the country and the gods within the ground?   1645
Oh, can Orestes live, be somewhere in sunlight still?
Shall fate grown gracious ever bring him back again
in strength of hand to overwhelm these murderers?

Aegisthus

You shall learn then, since you stick to stubbornness of mouth and hand.
Up now from your cover, my henchmen: here is work for you to do.   1650

Chorus

Look, they come! Let every man clap fist upon his hilted sword.

Aegisthus

I too am sword-handed against you; I am not afraid of death.

Chorus

Death you said and death it shall be; we take up the word of fate.

Clytaemestra

No, my dearest, dearest of all men, we have done enough. No more
violence. Here is a monstrous harvest and a bitter reaping time.   1655
There is pain enough already. Let us not be bloody now.
Honored gentlemen of Argos, go to your homes now and give way
to the stress of fate and season. We could not do otherwise
than we did. If this is the end of suffering, we can be content
broken as we are by the brute heel of angry destiny.   1660
Thus a woman speaks among you. Shall men deign to understand?

Aegisthus

Yes, but think of these foolish lips that blossom into leering gibes,
think of the taunts they spit against me daring destiny and power,
sober opinion lost in insults hurled against my majesty.

Chorus

It was never the Argive way to grovel at a vile man's feet.   1665

Aegisthus

I shall not forget this; in the days to come I shall be there.

Chorus

Nevermore, if God's hand guiding brings Orestes home again.

Aegisthus

Exiles feed on empty dreams of hope. I know it. I was one.

Chorus

Have your way, gorge and grow fat, soil justice, while the power is yours.

Aegisthus

You shall pay, make no mistake, for this misguided insolence.　　1670

Chorus

Crow and strut, brave cockerel by your hen; you have no threats to fear.

Clytaemestra

These are howls of impotent rage; forget them, dearest; you and I

have the power; we two shall bring good order to our house at least.

(*They enter the house. The doors close. All persons leave the stage.*)

PROMETHEUS BOUND

Translated by David Grene

INTRODUCTION

The date of this play is unknown. The other two tragedies which completed the trilogy are lost, and the arrangement is disputed. I give here the reconstruction which seems most plausible to me.

Prometheus Bound is the first play in the trilogy. It opens, of course, with the fastening of Prometheus to the rock, but a great deal of the body of the play is taken up with the explanation, through the hero's conversations with others, of how this punishment has come about. In the great revolution of the Olympians against their elders, the Titans, Prometheus, a Titan, went over to the side of the Olympians; it is, he claims, thanks to him that Olympian Zeus is now the master of the universe. But Prometheus outraged Zeus by befriending, against the plans of Zeus, the pitiful, rudimentary, experimental race of men. Therefore he is punished and, at the end, sunk beneath the earth, whence he will emerge only to face the new torment of the bird of prey which will feed upon his liver. The sequel, *Prometheus Unbound*, of which some fragments remain, would find Prometheus in his new agony. Heracles, the descendant of Io, frees him by killing the eagle. But his final reconciliation with Zeus, confidently predicted in *Prometheus Bound*, must be deferred to the totally lost *Prometheus the Firebearer*, last of the trilogy, which would end in his installation as a god of cult and the establishment of the ritual torch race which is partly in his honor.

The startling fact about *Prometheus Bound* is the cruel, almost villainous part played by Zeus. Although he never appears, his motives seem plain, and they are those of a tyrant. Romantic poets such as Goethe and Shelley welcomed this story as a parable of human revolt against autocracy and established religion. Others, seeing Aeschylus as a pious conservative, an awe-struck Zeus-man, have sometimes been so troubled as to deny that Aeschylus wrote the play at all. It is better to consider the drama, within its trilogy, not as a piece of theology but as a play, a story, using superhuman materials. For Prometheus, though overpowered, is a full immortal god, not a man. This use of an omniscient indestructible deity in

place of the faulted human hero presents its dramatic difficulties.
It makes the action static. But the ultimate reconciliation is not to
be forgotten.

TRANSLATOR'S NOTE

Originally, I had rendered much of this play in prose. I revised
the translation in 1990 and left in prose only the opening scene
between Might and Hermes with Violence and Prometheus as
mutae personae. This is very different in tone from anything else
in the *Prometheus,* and I finally thought that it might just be rendered in prose.

The majestic poetry is beyond the reach of anyone not so great
as the play's author.

CHARACTERS

Might

Violence (muta persona)

Hephaestus

Prometheus

Oceanos

Io

Hermes

Chorus of daughters of Oceanos

PROMETHEUS BOUND

SCENE: *A bare and desolate crag in the Caucasus. Enter Might and Violence, demons, servants of Zeus, and Hephaestus, the smith.*

Might

This is the world's limit that we have come to; this is the Scythian country, an untrodden desolation. Hephaestus, it is you that must heed the commands the Father laid upon you to nail this malefactor to the high craggy rocks in fetters unbreakable of adamantine chain. For it was your flower, the brightness of fire that devises all, that he stole and gave to mortal men; this is the sin for which he must pay the Gods the penalty—that he may learn to endure   10
and like the sovereignty of Zeus and quit his man-loving disposition.

Hephaestus

Might and Violence, in you the command of Zeus has its perfect fulfilment: in you there is nothing to stand in its way. But, for myself, I have not the heart to bind violently a God who is my kin here on this wintry cliff. Yet there is constraint upon me to have the heart for just that, for it is a dangerous thing to treat the Father's words lightly.

High-contriving Son of Themis of Straight Counsel: this is not of your will nor of mine; yet I shall nail you in bonds of indissoluble bronze on this crag far from men. Here you shall hear no voice   20
of mortal; here you shall see no form of mortal. You shall be grilled by the sun's bright fire and change the fair bloom of your skin. You shall be glad when Night comes with her mantle of stars and hides the sun's light; but the sun shall scatter the hoarfrost again at dawn. Always the grievous burden of your torture

will be there to wear you down; for he that shall cause it to cease
has yet to be born.

Such is the reward you reap of your man-loving disposition. For
you, a God, feared not the anger of the Gods, but gave honors to
mortals beyond what was just. Wherefore you shall mount guard   30
on this unlovely rock, upright, sleepless, not bending the knee.
Many a groan and many a lamentation you shall utter, but they
shall not serve you. For the mind of Zeus is hard to soften with
prayer and every ruler is harsh whose rule is new.

Might

Come, why are you holding back? Why are you pitying in vain?
Why is it that you do not hate a God whom the Gods hate most
of all? Why do you not hate him, since it was your honor that he
betrayed to men?

Hephaestus

Our kinship has strange power; that, and our life together.

Might

Yes. But to turn a deaf ear to the Father's words—how can that   40
be? Do you not fear that more?

Hephaestus

You are always pitiless, always full of ruthlessness.

Might

There is no good singing dirges over him. Do not labor uselessly
at what helps not at all.

Hephaestus

O handicraft of mine—that I deeply hate!

Might

Why do you hate it? To speak simply, your craft is in no way the
author of his present troubles.

Hephaestus

Yet would another had had this craft allotted to him.

Might
There is nothing without discomfort except the overlordship of the Gods. For only Zeus is free.   50

Hephaestus
I know. I have no answer to this.

Might
Hurry now. Throw the chain around him that the Father may not look upon your tarrying.

Hephaestus
There are the fetters, there: you can see them.

Might
Put them on his hands: strong, now with the hammer: strike. Nail him to the rock.

Hephaestus
It is being done now. I am not idling at my work.

Might
Hammer it more; put in the wedge; leave it loose nowhere. He's a cunning fellow at finding a way even out of hopeless difficulties.

Hephaestus
Look now, his arm is fixed immovably!   60

Might
Nail the other safe, that he may learn, for all his cleverness, that he is duller witted than Zeus.

Hephaestus
No one, save Prometheus, can justly blame me.

Might
Drive the obstinate jaw of the adamantine wedge right through his breast: drive it hard.

Hephaestus
Alas, Prometheus, I groan for your sufferings.

Might

Are you pitying again? Are you groaning for the enemies of
Zeus? Have a care, lest some day you may be pitying yourself.

Hephaestus

You see a sight that hurts the eye.

Might

I see this rascal getting his deserts. Throw the girth around his   70
sides.

Hephaestus

I am forced to do this; do not keep urging me.

Might

Yes, I will urge you, and hound you on as well. Get below now,
and hoop his legs in strongly.

Hephaestus

There now, the task is done. It has not taken long.

Might

Hammer the piercing fetters with all your power, for the Over-
seer of our work is severe.

Hephaestus

Your looks and the refrain of your tongue are alike.

Might

You can be softhearted. But do not blame my stubbornness and
harshness of temper.   80

Hephaestus

Let us go. He has the harness on his limbs.

Might (to Prometheus)

Now, play the insolent; now, plunder the Gods' privileges and give
them to creatures of a day. What drop of your sufferings can mortals
spare you? The Gods named you wrongly when they called you
Forethought; you yourself *need* Forethought to extricate yourself
from this contrivance.

(Prometheus is left alone on the rock.)

Prometheus

Bright light, swift-winged winds, springs of the rivers, number-
    less
laughter of the sea's waves, earth, mother of all, and the all-seeing   90
circle of the sun: I call upon you to see what I, a God, suffer
at the hands of Gods—
see with what kind of torture
worn down I shall wrestle ten thousand
years of time—
such is the despiteful bond that the Prince
has devised against me, the new Prince
of the Blessed Ones. Oh woe is me!
I groan for the present sorrow,
I groan for the sorrow to come, I groan
questioning when there shall come a time
when He shall ordain a limit to my sufferings.
What am I saying? I have known all before,   100
all that shall be, and clearly known; to me,
nothing that hurts shall come with a new face.
So must I bear, as lightly as I can,
the destiny that fate has given me;
for I know well against necessity,
against its strength, no one can fight and win.

I cannot speak about my fortune, cannot
hold my tongue either. It was mortal man
to whom I gave great privileges and
for that was yoked in this unyielding harness.
I hunted out the secret spring of fire
that filled the narthex stem, which when revealed   110
became the teacher of each craft to men,
a great resource. This is the sin committed
for which I stand accountant, and I pay
nailed in my chains under the open sky.

Ah! Ah!
What sound, what sightless smell approaches me,

God sent, or mortal, or mingled?
Has it come to earth's end
to look on my sufferings,
or what does it wish?
You see me a wretched God in chains,   120
the enemy of Zeus, hated of all
the Gods that enter Zeus's palace hall,
because of my excessive love for Man.
What is that? The rustle
of birds' wings near? The air whispers
with the gentle strokes of wings.
Everything that comes toward me is occasion for fear.

(*The Chorus, composed of the daughters of Oceanos, enters,
the members wearing some formalized representation of
wings, so that their general appearance is birdlike.*)

Chorus
　　Fear not: this is a company of friends
　　that comes to your mountain with swift
　　rivalry of wings.   130
　　Hardly have we persuaded our Father's
　　mind, and the quick-bearing winds
　　speeded us hither. The sound
　　of stroke of bronze rang through our cavern
　　in its depths and it shook from us
　　shamefaced modesty; unsandaled
　　we have hastened on our chariot of wings.

Prometheus
　　Alas, children of teeming Tethys and of him
　　who encircles all the world with stream unsleeping,
　　Father Ocean,   140
　　look, see with what chains
　　I am nailed on the craggy heights
　　of this gully to keep a watch
　　that none would envy me.

Chorus
I see, Prometheus: and a mist of fear and tears
besets my eyes as I see your form
wasting away on these cliffs
in adamantine bonds of bitter shame.
For new are the steersmen that rule Olympus:
and new are the customs by which Zeus rules,
customs that have no law to them,
but what was great before he brings to nothingness.   150

Prometheus
Would that he had hurled me
underneath the earth and underneath
the House of Hades, host to the dead—
yes, down to limitless Tartarus,
yes, though he bound me cruelly
in chains unbreakable,
so neither God nor any other being
might have found joy in gloating over me.
Now as I hang, the plaything of the winds,
my enemies can laugh at what I suffer.

Chorus
Who of the Gods is so hard of heart   160
that he finds joy in this?
Who is that that does not feel
sorrow answering your pain—
save only Zeus? For he malignantly,
always cherishing a mind
that bends not, has subdued the breed
of Ouranos, nor shall he cease
until he satisfies his heart,
or someone take the rule from him—that hard-to-capture rule—
by some device of subtlety.

Prometheus
Yes, there shall come a day for me
when he shall need me, me that now am tortured

in bonds and fetters—he shall need me then,
this president of the Blessed—   170
to show the new plot whereby he may be spoiled
of his throne and his power.
Then not with honeyed tongues
of persuasion shall he enchant me;
he shall not cow me with his threats
to tell him what I know,
until he free me from my cruel chains
and pay me recompense for what I suffer.

Chorus
   You are stout of heart, unyielding   180
   to the bitterness of pain.
   You are free of tongue, too free.
   It is my mind that piercing fear has fluttered;
   your misfortunes frighten me.
   Where and when is it fated
   to see you reach the term, to see you reach
   the harbor free of trouble at the last?
   A disposition none can win, a heart
   that no persuasions soften—these are his,
   the Son of Kronos.

Prometheus
   I know that he is savage: and his justice
   a thing he keeps by his own standard: still
   that will of his shall melt to softness yet   190
   when he is broken in the way I know,
   and though his temper now is oaken hard
   it shall be softened: hastily he'll come
   to meet my haste, to join in amity
   and union with me—one day he shall come.

Chorus
   Reveal it all to us; tell us the story,
   on what charges Zeus has laid hold on you

and tortures you so cruelly, with dishonor.
Instruct us if the telling will not harm you.

Prometheus
To speak of this is bitterness. To keep silent
bitter no less; and every way is misery.   200

When first the Gods began their angry quarrel,
and God matched God in rising faction, some
eager to drive old Kronos from his throne
that Zeus might rule—the fools!—others again
earnest that Zeus might never be their king—
I then with the best counsel tried to win
the Titans, sons of Ouranos and Earth,
but failed. They would have none of crafty schemes
and in their savage arrogance of spirit
thought they would lord it easily by force.   210
But she that was my mother, Themis, Earth—
she is but one although her names are many—
had prophesied to me how it should be,
even how the fates decreed it: and she said
that "not by strength nor overmastering force
the fates allowed the conquerors to conquer
but by guile only": This is what I told them,
but they would not vouchsafe a glance at me.
Then with those things before me it seemed best
to take my mother and join Zeus's side: 220
he was as willing as we were:
thanks to my plans the dark receptacle
of Tartarus conceals the ancient Kronos,
him and his allies. These were the services
I rendered to this tyrant and these pains
the payment he has given me in requital.
This is a sickness rooted and inherent
in the nature of a tyranny:
that he that holds it does not trust his friends.

But you have asked on what particular
charge he now tortures me: this I will tell you.
As soon as he ascended to the throne   230
that was his father's, straightway he assigned
to the several Gods their several privileges
and portioned out the power, but to the unhappy
breed of mankind he gave no heed, intending
to blot the race out and create a new.
Against these plans none stood save I: I dared.
I rescued men from shattering destruction
that would have carried them to Hades' house;
and therefore I am tortured on this rock,
a bitterness to suffer, and a pain
to pitiful eyes. I gave to mortal man   240
a precedence over myself in pity: I
can win no pity: pitiless is he
that thus chastises me, a spectacle
bringing dishonor on the name of Zeus.

Chorus
  Of iron mind he must be, must be made of stone
  who does not sympathize, Prometheus, with your sufferings.
  Myself, I would not have chosen to look on them;
  now that I do, my heart is full of pain.

Prometheus
  Yes, to my friends the sight is pitiable.

Chorus
  Did you perhaps go further than you have told us?

Prometheus
  Yes, I stopped mortals from foreseeing doom.   250

Chorus
  What cure did you discover for that sickness?

Prometheus
  I sowed in them blind hopes.

Chorus
  That was a great help that you gave to men.

Prometheus
Besides, I myself gave them fire.

Chorus
Do now creatures of a day own bright-faced fire?

Prometheus
Yes and from it they shall learn many crafts.

Chorus
So it was on such charges as this that Zeus—

Prometheus
Tortures me, gives me no respite from my pains.

Chorus
Is there no term prescribed for your suffering?

Prometheus
None save when it seems good to Zeus himself.   260

Chorus
How shall it seem good? What hope is there? Do you not see
that you were wrong? How you have been wrong, it is not
a pleasure for me to say, and pain for you.
Let us let all this be; seek some deliverance
out of your trial.

Prometheus
It is an easy thing for one whose foot
is on the outside of calamity
to give advice and to rebuke the sufferer.
I have known all that you have said: I knew,
I knew when I transgressed nor will deny it.
In helping man I brought my troubles on me;
but yet I did not think that with such tortures   270
I should be wasted on these airy cliffs,
this lonely mountain top, with no one near.
But do not sorrow for my present suffering;
alight on earth and hear what is to come
that you may know the whole complete: I beg you

alight and join your sorrow with mine: misfortune
wandering the same track lights now upon one
and now upon another.

Chorus

Willing our ears,
that hear you cry to them, Prometheus.   280
Now with light foot I leave the rushing car
and sky, the holy path of birds, and light
upon this jutting rock: I long
to hear your story to the end.

(Enter Oceanos, riding on a hippocamp, or sea monster.)

Oceanos

I come
on a long journey, speeding past the boundaries,
to visit you, Prometheus: with the mind
alone, no bridle needed, I direct
my swift-winged bird; my heart is sore
for your misfortunes; you know that. I think   290
that it is kinship makes me feel them so.
Besides, apart from kinship, there is no one
I hold in higher estimation: that
you soon shall know and know beside that in me
there is no mere word-kindness: tell me
how I can help you, and you will never say
that you have any friend more loyal to you
than Oceanos.

Prometheus

What do I see? Have you, too, come to gape   300
in wonder at this great display, my torture?
How did you have the courage to come here
to this land, this Iron Mother, leaving the stream
called after you and the rock-roofed, self-established
caverns? Was it to feast your eyes upon
the spectacle of my suffering and join
in pity for my pain? Now look and see

the sight, this friend of Zeus, that helped set up
his tyranny, and see what agonies
twist me, by his instructions!

Oceanos

Yes, I see,
Prometheus, and I want, indeed I do,
to advise you for the best, for all your cleverness.   310
Know yourself and reform your ways to new ways,
for new is he that rules among the Gods.
But if you throw about such angry words,
words that are whetted swords, soon Zeus will hear you,
even though his seat in glory is far removed,
and then your present multitude of pains
will seem like child's play. My poor friend, give up
this angry mood of yours and look for means
of getting yourself free of trouble. Maybe
what I say seems to you both old and commonplace;
but this is what you pay, Prometheus, for   320
that tongue of yours which talked so high and haughty:
you are not yet humble, still you do not yield
to your misfortunes, and you wish, indeed,
to add some more to them; now, if you follow
me as a schoolmaster you will not kick
against the pricks, seeing that he, the King,
that rules alone, is harsh and sends accounts
to no one's audit for the deeds he does.
Now I will go and try if I can free you:
do you be quiet, do not talk so much.
Since your mind is so subtle, don't you know   330
that a vain tongue is subject to correction?

Prometheus

I envy you, that you stand clear of blame,
yet shared and dared in everything with me!
Now let me be, and have no care for me.
Do what you will, Him you will not persuade;

He is not easily won over: look,
take care lest coming here to me should hurt you.

Oceanos
You are by nature better at advising
others than yourself. I take my cue
from deeds, not words. Do not withhold me now
when I am eager to go to Zeus. I'm sure,
I'm sure that he will grant this favor to me,   340
to free you from your chains.

Prometheus
I thank you and will never cease; for loyalty
is not what you are wanting in. Don't trouble,
for you will trouble to no purpose, and no help
to me—if it so be you want to trouble.
No, rest yourself, keep away from this thing;
because I am unlucky I would not,
for that, have everyone unlucky too.
No, for my heart is sore already when
I think about my brothers' fortunes—Atlas,   350
who stands to westward of the world, supporting
the pillar of earth and heaven on his shoulders,
a load that suits no shoulders; and the earthborn
dweller in caves Cilician, whom I saw
and pitied, hundred-headed, dreadful monster,
fierce Typho, conquered and brought low by force.
Once against all the Gods he stood, opposing,
hissing out terror from his grim jaws; his eyes
flashed gorgon glaring lightning as he thought
to sack the sovereign tyranny of Zeus;
but upon him came the unsleeping bolt
of Zeus, the lightning-breathing flame, down rushing,   360
which cast him from his high aspiring boast.
Struck to the heart, his strength was blasted dead
and burnt to ashes; now a sprawling mass
useless he lies, hard by the narrow seaway

pressed down beneath the roots of Aetna: high
above him on the mountain peak the smith
Hephaestus works at the anvil. Yet one day
there shall burst out rivers of fire, devouring
with savage jaws the fertile, level plains   370
of Sicily of the fair fruits; such boiling wrath
with weapons of fire-breathing surf, a fiery
unapproachable torrent, shall Typho vomit,
though Zeus's lightning left him but a cinder.
But all of this you know: you do not need me
to be your schoolmaster: reassure yourself
as you know how: this cup I shall drain myself
till the high mind of Zeus shall cease from anger.

Oceanos

    Do you not know, Prometheus,
    that words are doctors for a diseased temper?   380

Prometheus

    Yes, if in season due one soothes the heart,
    not violently reduces the swelling temper.

Oceanos

    In loyalty to you and courage to show it
    what penalty do you see for me? Now tell me.

Prometheus

    Only futile effort and a silly good nature.

Oceanos

    Suffer me to be sick of this complaint,
    for it is best for wise ones to seem foolish.

Prometheus

    The fault will seem to be mine if you do this.

Oceanos

    It is clear your words would send me home again.

Prometheus

    Yes, for lamenting now will lead to enmity.   390

Oceanos
> With him that now sits on the throne of power?

Prometheus
> His is a heart take heed you never vex.

Oceanos
> Your own misfortune, Prometheus, is my teacher.

Prometheus
> Off with you, then! Begone! Keep your present mind.

Oceanos
> These words of yours reach one who is ready to go.
> For my four-footed bird already paws
> the level track of heaven with his wings
> and gladly will he bend his knee
> in his home stable.

Chorus

STROPHE
> I cry aloud, Prometheus, and lament your bitter fate.
> My tender eyes are trickling tears: 400
> their fountains wet my cheek.
> This is a tyrant's deed; this is unlovely,
> a thing done by a tyrant's private laws,
> and with this thing Zeus shows his haughtiness
> of temper toward the Gods that were of old.

ANTISTROPHE
> Now all the earth has cried aloud, lamenting:
> now all that was magnificent of old
> laments your fall, laments your brethren's fall—   410
> as many as in holy Asia hold
> their stablished habitation, all lament
> in sympathy for your most grievous woes.

STROPHE
> Dwellers in the land of Colchis,
> maidens fearless in the fight,

and the host of Scythia, living
round the lake Maeotis, living
on the edges of the world.

ANTISTROPHE
And Arabia's flower of warriors   420
and the craggy fortress keepers
near Caucasian mountains, fighters
terrible, crying for battle,
brandishing sharp pointed spears.

STROPHE
One God and one God only I have seen
before this day, in torture and in bonds
unbreakable: he was a Titan,
Atlas, whose strength and might
ever exceeded; now he bends his back
and groans beneath the load of earth and heaven.   430

ANTISTROPHE
The wave cries out as it breaks into surf;
the depth cries out, lamenting you; the dark
Hades, the hollow underneath the world,
sullenly groans below; the springs
of sacred flowing rivers all lament
the pain and pity of your suffering.

Prometheus
Do not think from pride and stubbornness I am silent.
In self awareness my heart is eaten away
to see myself insulted as I am.
Yet to these new gods who but I assigned
their privileges of honor in full completion?   440
Of all that I say nothing, for I would speak
to you who know it. But man's tribulation,
that I would have you hear—how I found them mindless
and gave them minds, made them masters of their wits.
I will tell you this not as reproaching man,

but to set forth the goodwill of my gifts.
First they had eyes but had no eyes to see,
and ears but heard not. Like shapes within a dream
they dragged through their long lives and muddled all,
haphazardly. They knew not how to build   450
brick houses to face the sun, nor work in wood.
They lived beneath the earth like swarming ants
in sunless caves. They had no certain mark
of winter nor of flowery spring nor summer,
with its crops, but did all this without intelligence
until it was I that showed them—yes, it was I—
stars' risings and their settings hard to judge.
And numbering as well, preeminent
of subtle devices, and letter combinations
that hold all in memory, the Muses' mother skilled in craft,   460
I found for them. I was the first to yoke
beasts to be slave to the traces, and with their bodies
to be man's substitute in the hardest work. I harnessed
to the carriage horses obedient to the rein,
the crowning glory of the rich man's luxury.
And carriages that wander on the sea,
the ships sail-winged, who else but I invented?
Such, to my sorrow, were the devices which
I found for men, but have no clever means
to rid myself of the afflictions now oppressing me.   470

Chorus

You have suffered terribly. Bewildered in your mind
you are astray, and like a bad doctor who
has fallen sick, you have lost heart not finding
by what drugs your own disease is curable.

Prometheus

If you hear the rest, you will marvel even more
at what crafts and what resources I contrived.
Greatest was this: when one of mankind was sick,

there was no defense for him—neither healing food
nor drink nor unguent; for lack of drugs they wasted,
until I showed them blendings of mild simples
with which they drive away all kinds of sickness.   480
The many ways of prophesying I charted;
I was the one who first judged what out of dreams
came truly real; and for mankind I gave meaning
to ominous sounds, hard of interpretation,
and to the significance of road encounters.
The flights of hook-taloned birds I analyzed,
which of them were in nature prosperous
and lucky, and what manner of life each led,
their hates and loves, companionships with each other;   490
what smoothness of the entrails and what color
the gall should have if it were to please the Gods,
and also the dappled beauty of the lobe.
It was I bound the thighbones wrapped in fat,
and the long shank; it was I that set mortals on
the murky road of prophecy. Flaming signs
I made visible which till then were only dim.
So much for these things. Then beneath the earth   500
those hidden blessings for man, bronze, iron, silver
and gold—who can claim to have discovered before me?
No one, I am sure, who wants to speak to the purpose.
In one short sentence understand it all:
every art of mankind comes from Prometheus.

Chorus
  Do not help mortals beyond due occasion
  while careless of your own misfortune.
  For I am strong in hope that once released   510
  from these chains you will be no less strong than Zeus.

Prometheus
  These things the Fate that brings all to fulfilment
  has not yet determined that they be accomplished.

I must first be twisted by ten thousand pangs
and agonies before I escape my bondage.
Craft is far weaker than necessity.

Chorus
Who then is the steersman of necessity?

Prometheus
The three-formed Fates and the remembering Furies.

Chorus
And is Zeus, then, weaker than these?

Prometheus
                                        Yes,
for he too cannot escape what is fated.

Chorus
But what is fated for Zeus save rule eternal?

Prometheus
You cannot know that yet; do not entreat me.   520

Chorus
This must be a solemn secret that you veil.

Prometheus
Think of some other story; this is not seasonable
to utter; it must be wholly hidden.
For only by so keeping it can I
escape these shameful bonds and agonies.

Chorus

STROPHE
May Zeus never, Zeus that all
the universe controls, oppose
his power against *my* mind:
may I never dallying
be slow to give my worship at   530
the sacrificial feasts
when the bulls are killed beside
quenchless Father Ocean:

may I never sin in word:
may these precepts still abide
in my mind nor melt away.

ANTISTROPHE
It is a sweet thing to draw out
a long, long life in cheerful hopes,
and feed the spirit in the bright
benignity of happiness:
but I shiver when I see you   540
wasted with ten thousand pains,
all because you did not tremble
at the name of Zeus: your mind
was yours, not his, and at its bidding
you regarded mortal men
too high, Prometheus.

STROPHE
Kindness that cannot be requited, tell me,
where is the help in that, my friend? What succor
in creatures of a day? You did not see
the feebleness that draws its breath in gasps,
a dreamlike feebleness by which the race   550
of man is held in bondage, a blind prisoner.
So the plans of men shall never
pass the ordered law of Zeus.

ANTISTROPHE
This I have learned while I looked on your pains,
deadly pains, Prometheus.
A dirge for you came to my lips, so different
from the other song I sang to crown your marriage
in honor of your couching and your bath,
upon the day you won her with your gifts
to share your bed—of your own race she was,
Hesione—and so you brought her home.   560

(Enter Io, a girl wearing horns like an ox.)

Io

　　What land is this? what race of men? Who is it
　　I see here tortured in this rocky bondage?
　　What is the sin he's paying for? Oh tell me
　　to what part of the world my wanderings have brought me.
　　O, O, O,
　　there it is again, there again—it stings me,
　　the gadfly, the ghost of earth-born Argos:
　　keep it away, keep it away, earth!
　　I'm frightened when I see the shape of Argos,
　　Argos the herdsman with ten thousand eyes.　　　　　　　　570
　　He stalks me with his crafty eyes: he died,
　　but the earth didn't hide him; still he comes
　　even from the depths of the Underworld to hunt me:
　　he drives me starving by the sands of the sea.

　　The reed-woven pipe drones on in a hum
　　and drones and drones its sleep-giving strain:
　　O, O, O,
　　Where are you bringing me, my far-wandering wanderings?
　　Son of Kronos, what fault, what fault
　　did you find in me that you should yoke me
　　to a harness of misery like this,
　　that you should torture me so to madness　　　　　　　　580
　　driven in fear of the gadfly?

　　Burn me with fire: hide me in earth: cast me away
　　to monsters of the deep for food: but do not
　　grudge me the granting of this prayer, King.
　　Enough have my much wandering wanderings
　　exercised me: I cannot find
　　a way to escape my troubles.
　　Do you hear the voice of the cow-horned maid?

Prometheus

　　Surely I hear the voice of the gadfly-haunted
　　daughter of Inachus who fired with love　　　　　　　　590

the heart of Zeus and now through Hera's hate
is violently driven in courses overlong.

Io

How is it you speak my father's name?
Tell me, who are you? Who are you? Oh
who are you that so exactly accosts me by name?
You have spoken of the disease that the Gods have sent to me
which wastes me away, pricking with goads,
so that I am moving always
tortured and hungry, wild bounding,
quick sped I come,   600
a victim of jealous plots.
Some have been wretched
before me, but who of these
suffered as I do?
But declare to me clearly
what I have still to suffer: what would avail
against my sickness, what drug would cure it:
Tell me, if you know:
tell me, declare it to the unlucky, wandering maid.

Prometheus

I will tell you clearly all that you would know,
weaving no riddles, but in simple story
as it is just to open lips to friends.   610
You see Prometheus that gave fire to men.

Io

You that have shown yourself a common blessing
to all men, sad Prometheus, why are you punished?

Prometheus

I have but now ceased complaining of my sufferings.

Io

Will you grant me this favor?

Prometheus
  Say what it is
  you ask for. You will learn all from me.

Io
  Tell me who nailed you to this cliff.

Prometheus
                                    The plan
  was Zeus's, but it was Hephaestus' hand.

Io
  What was the offense for which this is punishment?   620

Prometheus
  Enough that I have told you clearly just so far.

Io
  Besides this, tell me the limit of my own wanderings.

Prometheus
  It were better not to know than to know this.

Io
  Do not hide from me what it is fated I should suffer.
  What shall its term be for this unhappy girl?

Prometheus
  It is not I grudge you this gift that you ask.

Io
  Then why not tell me everything at once.

Prometheus
  No grudging, but I dread to break your spirit.

Io
  Do not care for me more than I would have you.

Prometheus
  Since you are bent on it, I must speak; Now hear me, you.   630

Chorus
  Not yet. Give to me, too, a share of pleasure.
  Let us first question her about her sickness;

let herself tell us her disastrous chances.
Then let her be told by you what she must still suffer.

Prometheus

Io, it is your task to gratify
these spirits who are, moreover, your father's sisters.
To sorrow and make wail for your ill fortune,
when you will win a tear from those who listen,
is well worthwhile.

Io

I know not how I should distrust you: clearly   640
you shall hear all you want to know from me.
Yet even as I speak I groan in bitterness
for that storm sent by God on me, that ruin
of my beauty; I must sorrow when I think
who sent all this upon me. There were always
night visions that kept haunting me and coming
into my maiden chamber and exhorting
with winning words, "O maiden greatly blessed,
why are you still a maiden, you who might
make marriage with the greatest? Zeus is stricken
with lust for you; he is afire to try   650
the bed of love with you: do not disdain him.
Go, child, to Lerna's meadow, deep in grass,
to where your father's flocks and cattle stand,
that Zeus's eye may cease from longing for you."
With such dreams I was cruelly beset
night after night until I took the courage
to tell my father of my nightly terror.
He sent to Pytho many an embassy
and to Dodona seeking to discover
what deed or word of his might please the God,   660
but those he sent came back with riddling oracles
dark and beyond the power of understanding.
At last the word came clear to Inachus
charging him plainly that he cast me out

of home and country, drive me out footloose
to wander to the limits of the world;
if he should not obey, the oracle said,
the fire-faced thunderbolt would come from Zeus
and blot out his whole race. These were the oracles
of Loxias, and Inachus obeyed them.   670
He drove me out and shut his doors against me
with tears on both our parts, but Zeus's bit
compelled him to do this against his will.
Immediately my form and mind were changed
and all distorted; horned, as you see,
pricked on by the sharp biting gadfly, leaping
in frenzied jumps I ran beside the river
Kerchneia, good to drink, and Lerna's spring.
The earth-born herdsman Argos followed me
whose anger knew no limits, and he spied   680
after my tracks with all his hundred eyes.
Then an unlooked-for doom, descending suddenly,
took him from life: I, driven by the gadfly,
that god-sent scourge, was driven always onward
from one land to another: that is my story.
If you can tell me what remains for me,
tell me, and do not out of pity cozen
with kindly lies: there is no sickness worse
for me than words that to be kind must lie.

Chorus
    Hold! Keep away! Alas!
    never did I think that such strange
    words would come to my ears:
    never did I think such intolerable   690
    sufferings, an offense to the eye,
    shameful and frightening, so
    would chill my soul with a double-edged point.
    Alas, Alas, for your fate!
    I shudder when I look on Io's fortune.

Prometheus
  You groan too soon, you are full of fear too soon.
  Wait till you hear what still remains.

Chorus
  Speak, tell us to the end. For the sick it is sweet to know
  what pain is still to come and to know it clearly.

Prometheus
  The first request you made of me you gained   700
  lightly: from her you wished to hear the story
  of what she suffered. Now hear what remains,
  what sufferings this maid must yet endure
  from Hera. Do you listen, child of Inachus,
  hear and lay up my words within your heart
  that you may know the limits of your journey.
  First turn to the sun's rising and walk on
  over the fields no plough has broken: then
  you will come to the wandering Scythians,
  who live in wicker houses built above
  their well-wheeled wagons; they are an armed people,   710
  armed with the bow that strikes from far away:
  do not draw near them; rather let your feet
  touch the surf line of the sea where the waves moan,
  and cross their country: on your left there live
  the Chalybes who work with iron: these
  you must beware of; for they are not gentle,
  nor people whom a stranger dare approach.
  Then you will come to Insolence, a river
  that well deserves its name: but cross it not—
  It is no stream that you can easily ford—
  until you come to Caucasus itself,
  the highest mountains, where the river's strength   720
  gushes from its very temples. Cross these peaks,
  the neighbors of the stars, and take the road
  southward until you reach the Amazons,
  the race of women who hate men, who one day

shall live around Thermodon in Themiscyra
where Salmydessos, rocky jaw of the sea,
stands sailor-hating, stepmother of ships.
The Amazons will set you on your way
and gladly: you will reach Cimmeria,
the isthmus, at the narrow gates of the lake.   730
Leave this with a good heart and cross the channel,
the channel of Maeotis: and hereafter
for all time men shall talk about your crossing,
and they shall call the place for you Cow's-ford.*
Leave Europe's mainland then, and go to Asia.

(*To the Chorus*)
Do you now think this tyrant of the Gods
is hard in all things without difference?
He was a God and sought to lie in love
with this girl who was mortal, and on her
he brought this curse of wandering: bitter indeed
you found your marriage with this suitor, maid.
Yet you must think of all that I have told you
as still only in prelude.   740

Io
O, O!

Prometheus
Again you cry out, again you lament? What then
will you do when you learn your other sufferings?

Chorus
Is there still suffering that you have to tell her?

Prometheus
A wintry sea of agony and ruin.

*Cow's–ford: Bosporus

Io

What is the good of life to me? Why should I not
quickly dash myself down from this blind precipice
to strike the ground and win a quittance
of all my pains? Better at once to die   750
than suffer torment all the rest of my days.

Prometheus

You would find it hard to bear these trials of mine,
since for me death is not decreed at all.
Death would indeed be a riddance of my suffering,
but, as it is, there is no limit set
for pain, save when Zeus falls from his seat of power.

Io

Is there a time when Zeus shall fall?

Prometheus

You would be glad, I think, to see that end.

Io

How should I not, who suffer so cruelly from him?

Prometheus

Know surely, then, that this will come to pass.   760

Io

Who will despoil him of his sovereign power?

Prometheus

His own light-witted counsels will undo him.

Io

How? Tell me, if there is no harm in telling.

Prometheus

He will make a marriage which one day he will rue.

Io

With god or mortal? Tell me if it may be told.

Prometheus

Why tell what marriage? That may not be spoken.

Io

Will it be by his wife that he shall lose his throne?

Prometheus

Yes. She shall bear a son greater than his father.

Io

Can he not turn aside this doom of his?

Prometheus

No, save only by my release from bondage.   770

Io

But who will free you against Zeus's will?

Prometheus

That must be one of your own descendants.

Io

What! Will a child of mine free you one day?

Prometheus

Yes, in the generation tenth and third.

Io

No longer can I grasp your prophecy.

Prometheus

Then do not seek to know your own troubles further.

Io

Do not offer me the gift and then withhold it.

Prometheus

I will offer you the choice of the two stories.

Io

Which are they? Tell me, give me the choice.

Prometheus

Yes, I will give it you: either to tell you,   780
clearly, the rest of your troubles or my deliverer.

Chorus

Give *her* the one of the two and me the other,
a kindly favor. Do not deny the tale.

Tell her what still remains of her wanderings,
and me the deliverer. That is what I want.

Prometheus
    Since you have so much eagerness, I will not
refuse to tell you all that you have asked me.
First to you, Io, I shall tell the tale
of your sad wanderings, rich in groans—inscribe
the story in the tablets of your mind.   790
When you shall cross the channel that divides
Europe from Asia, turn to the rising sun,
to the burnt plains, sun-scorched; cross by the edge
of the foaming sea till you come to Gorgona,
to the flat stretches of Kisthene's country.
There live the ancient maids, children of Phorcys:
these swan-formed hags, with but one common eye,
single-toothed monsters, such as nowhere else
the sun's rays look on nor the moon by night.
Near are their winged sisters, the three Gorgons,
with snakes to bind their hair up, mortal-hating: 800
no mortal that but looks on them shall live:
these are the sentry guards I tell you of.
Hear, too, of yet another gruesome sight,
the sharp-toothed hounds of Zeus, that have no bark,
the vultures—them take heed of—and the host
of one-eyed Arimaspians, horse-riding,
that live around the spring which flows with gold,
the spring of Pluto's river: go not near them.
A land far off, a nation of black men,
these you shall come to, men who live hard by
the fountain of the sun where is the river
Aethiops—travel by his banks along   810
to a waterfall where from the Bibline hills
Nile pours his holy waters, pure to drink.
This river shall be your guide to the triangular
land of the Nile and there, by Fate's decree,
there, Io, you shall find your distant home,

a colony for you and your descendants.
If anything of this is still obscure
or difficult ask me again and learn
clearly: I have more leisure than I wish.

Chorus

If there is anything further or left over
you have to tell her of her deadly traveling,
tell her. If that is all, grant us again   820
the favor that we asked for earlier.
You remember?

Prometheus

The limit of her wanderings complete
she now has heard: but so that she may know
that she has not been listening to no purpose
I shall recount what she endured before
she came to us here: this I give as pledge,
a witness to the good faith of my words.
The great part of the story I omit
and come to the very boundary of your travels.
When you had come to the Molossian plains
around the sheer back of Dodona where   830
is the oracular seat of Zeus Thesprotian,
the talking oaks, a wonder past belief,
by them full clearly, in no riddling terms,
you were hailed glorious wife of Zeus that shall be:
does anything of this wake pleasant memories?
Then, goaded by the gadfly, on you hastened
to the great gulf of Rhea by the track
at the side of the sea: but in returning course
you were storm-driven back: in time to come
that inlet of the sea shall bear your name
and shall be called Ionian, a memorial   840
to all men of your journeying: these are proofs
for you, of how far my mind sees something farther
than what is visible: for what is left,

to you and you this I shall say in common,
taking up again the track of my old tale.
There is a city, furthest in the world,
Canobos, near the mouth and issuing point
of the Nile: there Zeus shall make you sound of mind
touching you with a hand that brings no fear,
and through that touch alone shall come your healing.   850
You shall bear Epaphos, dark of skin, his name
recalling Zeus's touch and his begetting.
This Epaphos shall reap the fruit of all
the land that is watered by the broad flowing Nile.
From him five generations, and again
to Argos they shall come, against their will,
in number fifty, women, flying from
a marriage with their kinsfolk: but these kinsfolk,
their hearts with lust aflutter like the hawks
barely outdistanced by the doves, will come
hunting a marriage that the law forbids:
the God shall grudge the men these women's bodies,
and the Pelasgian earth shall welcome them   860
in death: for death shall claim them in a fight
where women strike in the dark, a murderous vigil.
Each wife shall rob her husband of his life,
dipping in blood her two-edged sword: even so
may Love come, too, upon my enemies.
But one among these girls shall love beguile
from killing her bedfellow, blunting her purpose:
and she shall make her choice—to bear the name
of coward and not murderer: this girl
she shall in Argos bear a race of kings.
To tell this clearly needs a longer story,   870
but from her seed shall spring one brave and famous
for archery, and he shall set me free.
Such was the prophecy which ancient Themis,
my Titan mother, opened up to me;
but how and by what means it shall come true

would take too long to tell, and if you heard
the knowledge would not profit you.

Io

Eleleu, eleleu.
It creeps on me again, the twitching spasm,
the mind-destroying madness, burning me up,
and the gadfly's sting goads me on—
steel point by no fire tempered—   880
and my heart in its fear knocks on my breast.
There's a dazing whirl in my eyes as I run
out of my course by the madness driven,
the crazy frenzy; my tongue ungoverned
babbles, the words in a muddy flow strike
on the waves of the mischief I hate, strike wild
without aim or sense.

Chorus

STROPHE

A wise man indeed he was
that first in judgment weighed this word
and gave it tongue: the best by far
it is to marry in one's rank and station: 890
let no one working with her hands aspire
to marriage with those lifted high in pride
because of wealth, or of ancestral glory.

ANTISTROPHE

Never, never may you see me,
Fates majestic, drawing nigh
the bed of Zeus, to share it with the King,
nor ever may I know a heavenly wooer:
I dread such things beholding
Io's sad virginity
ravaged, ruined; bitter wandering
hers because of Hera's wrath.   900

EPODE

When a match has equal partners
then I fear not: may the eye
inescapable of the mighty
Gods not look on me.
That is a fight that none can fight: a fruitful
source of fruitlessness: I would not
know what I could do: I cannot
see the hope when Zeus is angry
of escaping him.

Prometheus

Yet shall this Zeus, for all his pride of heart,
be humble yet: such is the match he plans,
a marriage that shall drive him from his power
and from his throne, out of the sight of all.   910
So shall at last the final consummation
be brought about of Father Kronos' curse
which he, driven from his ancient throne, invoked
against the son deposing him: no one
of all the Gods save I alone can tell
a way to escape this mischief: I alone
know it and how. So let him confidently
sit on his throne and trust his heavenly thunder
and brandish in his hand his fiery bolt.
Nothing shall all of this avail against   920
a fall intolerable, a dishonored end.
So strong a wrestler Zeus is now equipping
against himself, a monster hard to fight.
This enemy shall find a plan to best
the thunderbolt, a thunderclap to best
the thunderclap of Zeus: and he shall shiver
Poseidon's trident, curse of sea and land.
So, in his crashing fall shall Zeus discover
how different are rule and slavery.

Chorus
You voice your wishes for the God's destruction.

Prometheus
They are my wishes, yet shall come to pass.

Chorus
Must we expect someone to conquer Zeus?   930

Prometheus
Yes, he shall suffer worse than I do now.

Chorus
Have you no fear of uttering such words?

Prometheus
Why should I fear, since death is not my fate?

Chorus
But he might give you pain still worse than this.

Prometheus
Then let him do so; all this I expect.

Chorus
Wise are the worshipers of Adrasteia.

Prometheus
Worship him, pray; flatter whatever king
is king today; but I care less than nothing
for Zeus. Let him do what he likes,
let him be king for his short time: he shall not   940
be king for long.
                Look, here is Zeus's footman,
this fetch-and-carry messenger of him,
the New King. Certainly he has come here
with news for us.

Hermes
                You, subtle-spirit, you
bitterly overbitter, you that sinned
against the immortals, giving honor to
the creatures of a day, you thief of fire:

the Father has commanded you to say
what marriage of his is this you brag about
that shall drive him from power—and declare it   950
in clear terms and no riddles. You, Prometheus,
do not cause me a double journey; these

(Pointing to the chains.)

will prove to you that Zeus is not softhearted.

Prometheus
Your speech is pompous sounding, full of pride,
as fits the lackey of the Gods. You are young
and young your rule and you think that the tower
in which you live is free from sorrow: from it
have I not seen two tyrants thrown? the third,
who now is king, I shall yet live to see him
fall, of all three most suddenly, most dishonored.
Do you think I will crouch before your Gods,   960
—so new—and tremble? I am far from that.
Hasten away, back on the road you came.
You shall learn nothing that you ask of me.

Hermes
Just such the obstinacy that brought you here,
to this self-willed calamitous anchorage.

Prometheus
Be sure of this: when I set my misfortune
against your slavery, I would not change.

Hermes
It is better, I suppose, to be a slave
to this rock, than Zeus's trusted messenger.

Prometheus
Thus must the insolent show their insolence!   970

Hermes
I think you find your present lot too soft.

Prometheus

Too soft? I would my enemies had it then,
and you are one of those I count as such.

Hermes

Oh, you would blame me too for your calamity?

Prometheus

In a single word, I am the enemy
of all the Gods that gave me ill for good.

Hermes

Your words declare you mad, and mad indeed.

Prometheus

Yes, if it's madness to detest my foes.

Hermes

No one could bear you in success.

Prometheus

                                    Alas!

Hermes

Alas! *Zeus* does not know that word.   980

Prometheus

Time in its aging course teaches all things.

Hermes

But you have not yet learned a wise discretion.

Prometheus

True: or I would not speak so to a servant.

Hermes

It seems you will not grant the Father's wish.

Prometheus

I should be glad, indeed, to requite his kindness!

Hermes

You mock me like a child!

Prometheus
                              And are you not
a child, and sillier than a child, to think
that I should tell you anything? There is not
a torture or an engine wherewithal
Zeus can induce me to declare these things,   990
till he has loosed me from these cruel shackles.
So let him hurl his smoky lightning flame,
and throw in turmoil all things in the world
with white-winged snowflakes and deep bellowing
thunder beneath the earth: me he shall not
bend by all this to tell him who is fated
to drive him from his tyranny.

Hermes
Think, here and now, if this seems to your interest.

Prometheus
I have already thought—and laid my plans.

Hermes
Bring your proud heart to know a true discretion—
O foolish spirit—in the face of ruin.   1000

Prometheus
You vex me by these senseless adjurations,
senseless as if you were to advise the waves.
Let it not cross your mind that I will turn
womanish-minded from my fixed decision
or that I shall entreat the one I hate
so greatly, with a woman's upturned hands,
to loose me from my chains: I am far from that.

Hermes
I have said too much already—so I think—
and said it to no purpose: you are not softened:
your purpose is not dented by my prayers.

You are a colt new broken, with the bit   1010
clenched in its teeth, fighting against the reins,
and bolting. You are far too strong and confident
in your weak cleverness. For obstinacy
standing alone is the weakest of all things
in one whose mind is not possessed by wisdom.
Think what a storm, a triple wave of ruin
will rise against you, if you will not hear me,
and no escape for you. First this rough crag
with thunder and the lightning bolt the Father
shall cleave asunder, and shall hide your body
wrapped in a rocky clasp within its depth;
a tedious length of time you must fulfil   1020
before you see the light again, returning.
Then Zeus's winged hound, the eagle red,
shall tear great shreds of flesh from you, a feaster
coming unbidden, every day: your liver
bloodied to blackness will be his repast.
And of this pain do not expect an end
until some God shall show himself successor
to take your tortures for himself and willing
go down to lightless Hades and the shadows
of Tartarus' depths. Bear this in mind
and so determine. This is no feigned boast   1030
but spoken with too much truth. The mouth of Zeus
does not know how to lie, but every word
brings to fulfilment. Look, you, and reflect
and never think that obstinacy is better
than prudent counsel.

Chorus
                         Hermes seems to us
to speak not altogether out of season.
He bids you leave your obstinacy and seek
a wise good counsel. Hearken to him. Shame
it were for one so wise to fall in error.

Prometheus

Before he told it me I knew this message: 1040
but there is no disgrace in suffering
at an enemy's hand, when you hate mutually.
So let the curling tendril of the fire
from the lightning bolt be sent against me: let
the air be stirred with thunderclaps, the winds
in savage blasts convulsing all the world.
Let earth to her foundations shake, yes to her root,
before the quivering storm: let it confuse
the paths of heavenly stars and the sea's waves
in a wild surging torrent: this my body
let Him raise up on high and dash it down   1050
into black Tartarus with rigorous
compulsive eddies: death he cannot give me.

Hermes

These are a madman's words, a madman's plan:
is there a missing note in this mad harmony?
is there a slack chord in his madness? You,
you, who are so sympathetic with his troubles,
away with you from here, quickly away!   1060
lest you should find your wits stunned by the thunder
and its hard defending roar.

Chorus

                      Say something else
different from this: give me some other counsel
that I will listen to: this word of yours
for all its instancy is not for us.
How dare you bid us practice baseness? We
will bear along with him what we must bear.
I have learned to hate all traitors: there is no
disease I spit on more than treachery.   1070

Hermes

Remember then my warning before the act:
when you are trapped by ruin don't blame fortune:

don't say that Zeus has brought you to calamity
that you could not foresee: do not do this:
but blame yourselves: now you know what you're doing:
and with this knowledge neither suddenly
nor secretly your own want of good sense
has tangled you in the net of ruin, past
all hope of rescue.

Prometheus
Now it is words no longer: now in very truth   1080
the earth is staggered: in its depths the thunder
bellows resoundingly, the fiery tendrils
of the lightning flash light up, and whirling clouds
carry the dust along: all the winds' blasts
dance in a fury one against the other
in violent confusion: earth and sea
are one, confused together: such is the storm
that comes against me manifestly from Zeus
to work its terrors. O Holy mother mine,   1090
O Sky that circling brings the light to all,
you see me, how I suffer, how unjustly.

OEDIPUS THE KING

Translated by David Grene

INTRODUCTION

The date is unknown. Most scholars are inclined to place it about 427 B.C., after the great plague at Athens, which is thought to have suggested the plague at Thebes in the play. But there is no reliable evidence. We happen to be told that this play, on its first presentation, gained only the second prize.

Aeschylus had already composed a Theban trilogy, of which an *Oedipus* (lost) was the second play, and we may assume that the largest outlines of the story were familiar to all. Or at least so much: that it was predicted that Oedipus would kill his father and marry his mother; that, unwittingly, he did both; and that these offenses were discovered and made public. Concerning details, there were certainly variations. There were different stories about how and where Oedipus died; Euripides in his lost *Oedipus* had the hero blinded by the henchmen of Laius; the traditions about Antigone and Ismene are not fixed.

Still, in *Oedipus the King*, once the hero appears and announces his identity, the audience will know the great glaring facts about Oedipus and will realize almost at once that Oedipus does not know these facts. The situation makes for a story heavily charged with irony. The advance of the action consists of a probing into the past. Every "act" or episode brings in a new "helper"—Oedipus himself, Creon, Teiresias, Jocasta, Messenger, Herdsman—each of whom contributes his clue, until the whole secret is out. A fresh dimension of irony lies in the fact that the ghastly tragedy is mounted on the frame of a happy romance—the lost baby miraculously saved, thought dead but restored and *united with his parents*. The search for the murderer of Laius and the identity of Oedipus come out at the same point. The discovery is the climax.

It would be difficult to interpret *Oedipus the King* as a story of the punishment of pride. The deeds for which the hero would be "punished" were preordained before he was even conceived. But it is true that the endowments which make him grand—his impulsive intellect, his passion for truth, his great physical strength, his integrity, and his pride—are all necessarily used to work out the pattern of his fate down to its final fulfilment in the realization of what that fate has been.

Even among the plays of Sophocles, *Oedipus the King* stands out for its poetry, the sinewy, intense composition of the spoken passages, and the wild splendor of the choral odes.

CHARACTERS

Oedipus, King of Thebes

Jocasta, His Wife

Creon, His Brother-in-Law

Teiresias, an Old Blind Prophet

A Priest

First Messenger

Second Messenger

A Herdsman

A Chorus of Old Men of Thebes

OEDIPUS THE KING

SCENE: *In front of the palace of Oedipus at Thebes. To the right of the stage near the altar stands the Priest with a crowd of children. Oedipus emerges from the central door.*

Oedipus

Children, young sons and daughters of old Cadmus,
why do you sit here with your suppliant crowns?
The town is heavy with a mingled burden
of sounds and smells, of groans and hymns and incense;   5
I did not think it fit that I should hear
of this from messengers but came myself,—
I Oedipus whom all men call the Great.

(*He turns to the Priest.*)

You're old and they are young; come, speak for them.
What do you fear or want, that you sit here   10
suppliant? Indeed I'm willing to give all
that you may need; I would be very hard
should I not pity suppliants like these.

Priest

O ruler of my country, Oedipus,
you see our company around the altar;   15
you see our ages; some of us, like these,
who cannot yet fly far, and some of us
heavy with age; these children are the chosen
among the young, and I the priest of Zeus.
Within the market place sit others crowned   20
with suppliant garlands, at the double shrine
of Pallas and the temple where Ismenus
gives oracles by fire. King, you yourself
have seen our city reeling like a wreck
already; it can scarcely lift its prow
out of the depths, out of the bloody surf.

A blight is on the fruitful plants of the earth, 25
A blight is on the cattle in the fields,
a blight is on our women that no children
are born to them; a God that carries fire,
a deadly pestilence, is on our town,
strikes us and spares not, and the house of Cadmus
is emptied of its people while black Death
grows rich in groaning and in lamentation. 30
We have not come as suppliants to this altar
because we thought of you as of a God,
but rather judging you the first of men
in all the chances of this life and when
we mortals have to do with more than man.
You came and by your coming saved our city, 35
freed us from tribute which we paid of old
to the Sphinx, cruel singer. This you did
in virtue of no knowledge we could give you,
in virtue of no teaching; it was God
that aided you, men say, and you are held
with God's assistance to have saved our lives.
Now Oedipus, Greatest in all men's eyes, 40
here falling at your feet we all entreat you,
find us some strength for rescue.
Perhaps you'll hear a wise word from some God,
perhaps you will learn something from a man
(for I have seen that for the skilled of practice
the outcome of their counsels live the most). 45
Noblest of men, go, and raise up our city,
go,—and give heed. For now this land of ours
calls you its savior since you saved it once.
So, let us never speak about your reign
as of a time when first our feet were set
secure on high, but later fell to ruin. 50
Raise up our city, save it and raise it up.
Once you have brought us luck with happy omen;
be no less now in fortune.

If you will rule this land, as now you rule it,
better to rule it full of men than empty.
For neither tower nor ship is anything
when empty, and none live in it together.

Oedipus

I pity you, children. You have come full of longing,
but I have known the story before you told it
only too well. I know you are all sick,
yet there is not one of you, sick though you are,
that is as sick as I myself.
Your several sorrows each have single scope
and touch but one of you. My spirit groans
for city and myself and you at once.
You have not roused me like a man from sleep;
know that I have given many tears to this,
gone many ways wandering in thought,
but as I thought I found only one remedy
and that I took. I sent Menoeceus' son
Creon, Jocasta's brother, to Apollo,
to his Pythian temple,
that he might learn there by what act or word
I could save this city. As I count the days,
it vexes me what ails him; he is gone
far longer than he needed for the journey.
But when he comes, then, may I prove a villain,
if I shall not do all the God commands.

Priest

Thanks for your gracious words. Your servants here
signal that Creon is this moment coming.

Oedipus

His face is bright. O holy Lord Apollo,
grant that his news too may be bright for us
and bring us safety.

55

60

65

70

75

80

Priest

It is happy news,
I think, for else his head would not be crowned
with sprigs of fruitful laurel.

Oedipus

We will know soon,
he's within hail. Lord Creon, my good brother, 85
what is the word you bring us from the God?

(Creon enters.)

Creon

A good word,—for things hard to bear themselves
if in the final issue all is well
I count complete good fortune.

Oedipus

What do you mean?
What you have said so far
leaves me uncertain whether to trust or fear. 90

Creon

If you will hear my news before these others
I am ready to speak, or else to go within.

Oedipus

Speak it to all;
the grief I bear, I bear it more for these
than for my own heart.

Creon

I will tell you, then, 95
what I heard from the God.
King Phoebus in plain words commanded us
to drive out a pollution from our land,
pollution grown ingrained within the land;
drive it out, said the God, not cherish it,
till it's past cure.

Oedipus

What is the rite
of purification? How shall it be done?

Creon

By banishing a man, or expiation   100
of blood by blood, since it is murder guilt
which holds our city in this destroying storm.

Oedipus

Who is this man whose fate the God pronounces?

Creon

My Lord, before you piloted the state
we had a king called Laius.

Oedipus

I know of him by hearsay. I have not seen him.   105

Creon

The God commanded clearly: let some one
punish with force this dead man's murderers.

Oedipus

Where are they in the world? Where would a trace
of this old crime be found? It would be hard
to guess where.

Creon

                                   The clue is in this land;   110
that which is sought is found;
the unheeded thing escapes:
so said the God.

Oedipus

                              Was it at home,
or in the country that death came upon him,
or in another country travelling?

Creon

He went, he said himself, upon an embassy,
but never returned when he set out from home.   115

Oedipus

Was there no messenger, no fellow traveller
who knew what happened? Such a one might tell
something of use.

Creon
> They were all killed save one. He fled in terror
> and he could tell us nothing in clear terms
> of what he knew, nothing, but one thing only.

Oedipus
> What was it?   120
> If we could even find a slim beginning
> in which to hope, we might discover much.

Creon
> This man said that the robbers they encountered
> were many and the hands that did the murder
> were many; it was no man's single power.

Oedipus
> How could a robber dare a deed like this
> were he not helped with money from the city,
> money and treachery?   125

Creon
>   That indeed was thought.
> But Laius was dead and in our trouble
> there was none to help.

Oedipus
> What trouble was so great to hinder you
> inquiring out the murder of your king?

Creon
> The riddling Sphinx induced us to neglect   130
> mysterious crimes and rather seek solution
> of troubles at our feet.

Oedipus
> I will bring this to light again. King Phoebus
> fittingly took this care about the dead,
> and you too fittingly.
> And justly you will see in me an ally,   135
> a champion of my country and the God.
> For when I drive pollution from the land

I will not serve a distant friend's advantage,
but act in my own interest. Whoever
he was that killed the king may readily
wish to dispatch me with his murderous hand;   140
so helping the dead king I help myself.

Come, children, take your suppliant boughs and go;
up from the altars now. Call the assembly
and let it meet upon the understanding
that I'll do everything. God will decide   145
whether we prosper or remain in sorrow.

Priest
Rise, children—it was this we came to seek,
which of himself the king now offers us.
May Phoebus who gave us the oracle
come to our rescue and stay the plague.   150

(Exeunt all but the Chorus.)

Chorus
    Strophe
What is the sweet spoken word of God from the shrine of Pytho
    rich in gold
that has come to glorious Thebes?
I am stretched on the rack of doubt, and terror and trembling
    hold
my heart, O Delian Healer, and I worship full of fears
for what doom you will bring to pass, new or renewed in the   155
    revolving years.
Speak to me, immortal voice,
child of golden Hope.

    Antistrophe
First I call on you, Athene, deathless daughter of Zeus,
and Artemis, Earth Upholder,   160
who sits in the midst of the market place in the throne which
    men call Fame,
and Phoebus, the Far Shooter, three averters of Fate,

come to us now, if ever before, when ruin rushed upon the state,   165
you drove destruction's flame away
out of our land.

Strophe
Our sorrows defy number;
all the ship's timbers are rotten;
taking of thought is no spear for the driving away of the plague.   170
There are no growing children in this famous land;
there are no women bearing the pangs of childbirth.
You may see them one with another, like birds swift on the
    wing,   175
quicker than fire unmastered,
speeding away to the coast of the Western God.

Antistrophe
In the unnumbered deaths
of its people the city dies;
those children that are born lie dead on the naked earth
unpitied, spreading contagion of death; and grey haired mothers
    and wives
everywhere stand at the altar's edge, suppliant, moaning;   182–85
the hymn to the healing God rings out but with it the wailing
    voices are blended.
From these our sufferings grant us, O golden Daughter of Zeus,
glad-faced deliverance.

Strophe
There is no clash of brazen shields but our fight is with the War
    God,
a War God ringed with the cries of men, a savage God who burns   191
    us;
grant that he turn in racing course backwards out of our coun-
    try's bounds
to the great palace of Amphitrite or where the waves of the   195
    Thracian sea
deny the stranger safe anchorage.
Whatsoever escapes the night

at last the light of day revisits;
so smite the War God, Father Zeus,
beneath your thunderbolt,
for you are the Lord of the lightning, the lightning that
    carries fire.   200

  Antistrophe
  And your unconquered arrow shafts, winged by the golden
    corded bow,
Lycean King, I beg to be at our side for help;   205
and the gleaming torches of Artemis with which she scours the
    Lycean hills,
and I call on the God with the turban of gold, who gave his name
    to this country of ours,   210
the Bacchic God with the wind flushed face,
Evian One, who travel
with the Maenad company,
combat the God that burns us
with your torch of pine;
for the God that is our enemy is a God unhonoured among the   215
    Gods.

                                     (*Oedipus returns.*)

Oedipus
  For what you ask me—if you will hear my words,
and hearing welcome them and fight the plague,
you will find strength and lightening of your load.

Hark to me; what I say to you, I say
as one that is a stranger to the story
as stranger to the deed. For I would not   220
be far upon the track if I alone
were tracing it without a clue. But now,
since after all was finished, I became
a citizen among you, citizens—
now I proclaim to all the men of Thebes:
who so among you knows the murderer   225
by whose hand Laius, son of Labdacus,

died—I command him to tell everything
to me,—yes, though he fears himself to take the blame
on his own head; for bitter punishment
he shall have none, but leave this land unharmed.
Or if he knows the murderer, another,   230
a foreigner, still let him speak the truth.
For I will pay him and be grateful, too.
But if you shall keep silence, if perhaps
some one of you, to shield a guilty friend,
or for his own sake shall reject my words—   235
hear what I shall do then:
I forbid that man, whoever he be, my land,
my land where I hold sovereignty and throne;
and I forbid any to welcome him
or cry him greeting or make him a sharer   240
in sacrifice or offering to the Gods,
or give him water for his hands to wash.
I command all to drive him from their homes,
since he is our pollution, as the oracle
of Pytho's God proclaimed him now to me.
So I stand forth a champion of the God
and of the man who died.   245
Upon the murderer I invoke this curse—
whether he is one man and all unknown,
or one of many—may he wear out his life
in misery to miserable doom!
If with my knowledge he lives at my hearth   250
I pray that I myself may feel my curse.
On you I lay my charge to fulfill all this
for me, for the God, and for this land of ours
destroyed and blighted, by the God forsaken.

Even were this no matter of God's ordinance   255
it would not fit you so to leave it lie,
unpurified, since a good man is dead
and one that was a king. Search it out.

Since I am now the holder of his office,
and have his bed and wife that once was his,   260
and had his line not been unfortunate
we would have common children—(fortune leaped
upon his head)—because of all these things,
I fight in his defence as for my father,
and I shall try all means to take the murderer   265
of Laius the son of Labdacus
the son of Polydorus and before him
of Cadmus and before him of Agenor.
Those who do not obey me, may the Gods
grant no crops springing from the ground they plough   270
nor children to their women! May a fate
like this, or one still worse than this consume them!
For you whom these words please, the other Thebans,
may Justice as your ally and all the Gods
live with you, blessing you now and for ever!   275

Chorus

As you have held me to my oath, I speak:
I neither killed the king nor can declare
the killer; but since Phoebus set the quest
it is his part to tell who the man is.

Oedipus

Right; but to put compulsion on the Gods   280
against their will—no man can do that.

Chorus

May I then say what I think second best?

Oedipus

If there's a third best, too, spare not to tell it.

Chorus

I know that what the Lord Teiresias
sees, is most often what the Lord Apollo   285
sees. If you should inquire of this from him
you might find out most clearly.

Oedipus
    Even in this my actions have not been sluggard.
    On Creon's word I have sent two messengers
    and why the prophet is not here already
    I have been wondering.

Chorus
                              His skill apart   290
    there is besides only an old faint story.

Oedipus
    What is it?
    I look at every story.

Chorus
                              It was said
    that he was killed by certain wayfarers.

Oedipus
    I heard that, too, but no one saw the killer.

Chorus
    Yet if he has a share of fear at all,
    his courage will not stand firm, hearing your curse.   295

Oedipus
    The man who in the doing did not shrink
    will fear no word.

Chorus
                              Here comes his prosecutor:
    led by your men the godly prophet comes
    in whom alone of mankind truth is native.

                    (*Enter Teiresias, led by a little boy.*)

Oedipus
    Teiresias, you are versed in everything,   300
    things teachable and things not to be spoken,
    things of the heaven and earth-creeping things.
    You have no eyes but in your mind you know
    with what a plague our city is afflicted.
    My lord, in you alone we find a champion,

in you alone one that can rescue us.
Perhaps you have not heard the messengers,   305
but Phoebus sent in answer to our sending
an oracle declaring that our freedom
from this disease would only come when we
should learn the names of those who killed King Laius,
and kill them or expel from our country.
Do not begrudge us oracles from birds,   310
or any other way of prophecy
within your skill; save yourself and the city,
save me; redeem the debt of our pollution
that lies on us because of this dead man.
We are in your hands; pains are most nobly taken
to help another when you have means and power.   315

Teiresias
Alas, how terrible is wisdom when
it brings no profit to the man that's wise!
This I knew well, but had forgotten it,
else I would not have come here.

Oedipus
                              What is this?
How sad you are now you have come!

Teiresias
                              Let me
go home. It will be easiest for us both   320
to bear our several destinies to the end
if you will follow my advice.

Oedipus
                              You'd rob us
of this your gift of prophecy? You talk
as one who had no care for law nor love
for Thebes who reared you.

Teiresias
Yes, but I see that even your own words
miss the mark; therefore I must fear for mine.   325

Oedipus

    For God's sake if you know of anything,
    do not turn from us; all of us kneel to you,
    all of us here, your suppliants.

Teiresias

    All of you here know nothing. I will not
    bring to the light of day my troubles, mine—
    rather than call them yours.

Oedipus

                What do you mean?
    You know of something but refuse to speak.   330
    Would you betray us and destroy the city?

Teiresias

    I will not bring this pain upon us both,
    neither on you nor on myself. Why is it
    you question me and waste your labour? I
    will tell you nothing.

Oedipus

    You would provoke a stone! Tell us, you villain,   335
    tell us, and do not stand there quietly
    unmoved and balking at the issue.

Teiresias

    You blame my temper but you do not see
    your own that lives within you; it is me
    you chide.

Oedipus

    Who would not feel his temper rise
    at words like these with which you shame our city?   340

Teiresias

    Of themselves things will come, although I hide them
    and breathe no word of them.

Oedipus

                Since they will come
    tell them to me.

Teiresias
                    I will say nothing further.
Against this answer let your temper rage
as wildly as you will.

Oedipus
                    Indeed I am   345
so angry I shall not hold back a jot
of what I think. For I would have you know
I think you were complotter of the deed
and doer of the deed save in so far
as for the actual killing. Had you had eyes
I would have said alone you murdered him.

Teiresias
Yes? Then I warn you faithfully to keep   350
the letter of your proclamation and
from this day forth to speak no word of greeting
to these nor me; you are the land's pollution.

Oedipus
How shamelessly you started up this taunt!
How do you think you will escape?   355

Teiresias
                    I have.
I have escaped; the truth is what I cherish
and that's my strength.

Oedipus
                    And who has taught you truth?
Not your profession surely!

Teiresias
                    You have taught me,
for you have made me speak against my will.

Oedipus
Speak what? Tell me again that I may learn it better.

Teiresias
Did you not understand before or would you
provoke me into speaking?   360

Oedipus
                    I did not grasp it,
  not so to call it known. Say it again.

Teiresias
  I say you are the murderer of the king
  whose murderer you seek.

Oedipus
                        Not twice you shall
  say calumnies like this and stay unpunished.

Teiresias
  Shall I say more to tempt your anger more?

Oedipus
  As much as you desire; it will be said   365
  in vain.

Teiresias
              I say that with those you love best
  you live in foulest shame unconsciously
  and do not see where you are in calamity.

Oedipus
  Do you imagine you can always talk
  like this, and live to laugh at it hereafter?

Teiresias
  Yes, if the truth has anything of strength.

Oedipus
  It has, but not for you; it has no strength   370
  for you because you are blind in mind and ears
  as well as in your eyes.

Teiresias
                    You are a poor wretch
  to taunt me with the very insults which
  every one soon will heap upon yourself.

Oedipus
  Your life is one long night so that you cannot
  hurt me or any other who sees the light.   375

Teiresias

    It is not fate that I should be your ruin,
    Apollo is enough; it is his care
    to work this out.

Oedipus

                     Was this your own design
    or Creon's?

Teiresias

                   Creon is no hurt to you,
    but you are to yourself.

Oedipus

    Wealth, sovereignty and skill outmatching skill   380
    for the contrivance of an envied life!
    Great store of jealousy fill your treasury chests,
    if my friend Creon, friend from the first and loyal,   385
    thus secretly attacks me, secretly
    desires to drive me out and secretly
    suborns this juggling, trick devising quack,
    this wily beggar who has only eyes
    for his own gains, but blindness in his skill.
    For, tell me, where have you seen clear, Teiresias,   390
    with your prophetic eyes? When the dark singer,
    the sphinx, was in your country, did you speak
    word of deliverance to its citizens?
    And yet the riddle's answer was not the province
    of a chance comer. It was a prophet's task
    and plainly you had no such gift of prophecy   395
    from birds nor otherwise from any God
    to glean a word of knowledge. But I came,
    Oedipus, who knew nothing, and I stopped her.
    I solved the riddle by my wit alone.
    Mine was no knowledge got from birds. And now
    you would expel me,
    because you think that you will find a place   400
    by Creon's throne. I think you will be sorry,

both you and your accomplice, for your plot
to drive me out. And did I not regard you
as an old man, some suffering would have taught you
that what was in your heart was treason.

Chorus

We look at this man's words and yours, my king,
and we find both have spoken them in anger.   405
We need no angry words but only thought
how we may best hit the God's meaning for us.

Teiresias

If you are king, at least I have the right
no less to speak in my defence against you.
Of that much I am master. I am no slave   410
of yours, but Loxias', and so I shall not
enroll myself with Creon for my patron.
Since you have taunted me with being blind,
here is my word for you.
You have your eyes but see not where you are
in sin, nor where you live, nor whom you live with.
Do you know who your parents are? Unknowing   415
you are an enemy to kith and kin
in death, beneath the earth, and in this life.
A deadly footed, double striking curse,
from father and mother both, shall drive you forth
out of this land, with darkness on your eyes,
that now have such straight vision. Shall there be
a place will not be harbour to your cries,   420
a corner of Cithaeron will not ring
in echo to your cries, soon, soon,—
when you shall learn the secret of your marriage,
which steered you to a haven in this house,—
haven no haven, after lucky voyage?
And of the multitude of other evils
establishing a grim equality
between you and your children, you know nothing.   425

So, muddy with contempt my words and Creon's!
Misery shall grind no man as it will you.

Oedipus

Is it endurable that I should hear
such words from him? Go and a curse go with you!   430
Quick, home with you! Out of my house at once!

Teiresias

I would not have come either had you not called me.

Oedipus

I did not know then you would talk like a fool—
or it would have been long before I called you.

Teiresias

I am a fool then, as it seems to you—   435
but to the parents who have bred you, wise.

Oedipus

What parents? Stop! Who are they of all the world?

Teiresias

This day will show your birth and will destroy you.

Oedipus

How needlessly your riddles darken everything.

Teiresias

But it's in riddle answering you are strongest.   440

Oedipus

Yes. Taunt me where you will find me great.

Teiresias

It is this very luck that has destroyed you.

Oedipus

I do not care, if it has saved this city.

Teiresias

Well, I will go. Come, boy, lead me away.

Oedipus

Yes, lead him off. So long as you are here,   445

you'll be a stumbling block and a vexation;
once gone, you will not trouble me again.

Teiresias
                                   I have said
what I came here to say not fearing your
countenance: there is no way you can hurt me.
I tell you, king, this man, this murderer
(whom you have long declared you are in search of,
indicting him in threatening proclamation   450
as murderer of Laius)—he is here.
In name he is a stranger among citizens
but soon he will be shown to be a citizen
true native Theban, and he'll have no joy
of the discovery: blindness for sight
and beggary for riches his exchange,   455
he shall go journeying to a foreign country
tapping his way before him with a stick.
He shall be proved father and brother both
to his own children in his house; to her
that gave him birth, a son and husband both;
a fellow sower in his father's bed
with that same father that he murdered.
Go within, reckon that out, and if you find me   460
mistaken, say I have no skill in prophecy.

(*Exeunt separately Teiresias and Oedipus.*)

Chorus
    Strophe
Who is the man proclaimed
by Delphi's prophetic rock
as the bloody handed murderer,   465
the doer of deeds that none dare name?
Now is the time for him to run
with a stronger foot
than Pegasus
for the child of Zeus leaps in arms upon him   470
with fire and the lightning bolt,

and terribly close on his heels
are the Fates that never miss.

Antistrophe
Lately from snowy Parnassus
clearly the voice flashed forth,
bidding each Theban track him down,   475
the unknown murderer.
In the savage forests he lurks and in
the caverns like
the mountain bull.
He is sad and lonely, and lonely his feet
that carry him far from the navel of earth;   480
but its prophecies, ever living,
flutter around his head.

Strophe
The augur has spread confusion,
terrible confusion;
I do not approve what was said   485
nor can I deny it.
I do not know what to say;
I am in a flutter of foreboding;
I never heard in the present
nor past of a quarrel between   490
the sons of Labdacus and Polybus,
that I might bring as proof
in attacking the popular fame
of Oedipus, seeking
to take vengeance for undiscovered
death in the line of Labdacus.   495

Antistrophe
Truly Zeus and Apollo are wise
and in human things all knowing;
but amongst men there is no   500
distinct judgment, between the prophet
and me—which of us is right.

One man may pass another in wisdom
but I would never agree
with those that find fault with the king
till I should see the word
proved right beyond doubt. For once
in visible form the Sphinx
came on him and all of us
saw his wisdom and in that test
he saved the city. So he will not be condemned by my mind.   512

(*Enter Creon.*)

Creon

Citizens, I have come because I heard
deadly words spread about me, that the king
accuses me. I cannot take that from him.
If he believes that in these present troubles   515
he has been wronged by me in word or deed
I do not want to live on with the burden
of such a scandal on me. The report   520
injures me doubly and most vitally—
for I'll be called a traitor to my city
and traitor also to my friends and you.

Chorus

Perhaps it was a sudden gust of anger
that forced that insult from him, and no judgment.

Creon

But did he say that it was in compliance   525
with schemes of mine that the seer told him lies?

Chorus

Yes, he said that, but why, I do not know.

Creon

Were his eyes straight in his head? Was his mind right
when he accused me in this fashion?

Chorus

I do not know; I have no eyes to see   530
what princes do. Here comes the king himself.

(Enter Oedipus.)

Oedipus
You, sir, how is it you come here? Have you so much
brazen-faced daring that you venture in
my house although you are proved manifestly
the murderer of that man, and though you tried,
openly, highway robbery of my crown?   535
For God's sake, tell me what you saw in me,
what cowardice or what stupidity,
that made you lay a plot like this against me?
Did you imagine I should not observe
the crafty scheme that stole upon me or
seeing it, take no means to counter it?   540
Was it not stupid of you to make the attempt,
to try to hunt down royal power without
the people at your back or friends? For only
with the people at your back or money can
the hunt end in the capture of a crown.

Creon
Do you know what you're doing? Will you listen
to words to answer yours, and then pass judgment?

Oedipus
You're quick to speak, but I am slow to grasp you,   545
for I have found you dangerous,—and my foe.

Creon
First of all hear what I shall say to that.

Oedipus
At least don't tell me that you are not guilty.

Creon
If you think obstinacy without wisdom
a valuable possession, you are wrong.   550

Oedipus
And you are wrong if you believe that one,
a criminal, will not be punished only
because he is my kinsman.

Creon

                              This is but just—
but tell me, then, of what offense I'm guilty?

Oedipus

Did you or did you not urge me to send   555
to this prophetic mumbler?

Creon

                    I did indeed,
and I shall stand by what I told you.

Oedipus

How long ago is it since Laius. . . .

Creon

What about Laius? I don't understand.

Oedipus

Vanished—died—was murdered?   560

Creon

                              It is long,
a long, long time to reckon.

Oedipus

                    Was this prophet
in the profession then?

Creon

                    He was, and honoured
as highly as he is today.

Oedipus

At that time did he say a word about me?

Creon

Never, at least when I was near him.   565

Oedipus

You never made a search for the dead man?

Creon

We searched, indeed, but never learned of anything.

Oedipus

Why did our wise old friend not say this then?

Creon

    I don't know; and when I know nothing, I
usually hold my tongue.

Oedipus

                You know this much,   570
and can declare this much if you are loyal.

Creon

    What is it? If I know, I'll not deny it.

Oedipus

    That he would not have said that I killed Laius
had he not met you first.

Creon

                You know yourself
whether he said this, but I demand that I   575
should hear as much from you as you from me.

Oedipus

    Then hear,—I'll not be proved a murderer.

Creon

    Well, then. You're married to my sister.

Oedipus

             Yes,
that I am not disposed to deny.

Creon

             You rule
this country giving her an equal share
in the government?

Oedipus

            Yes, everything she wants   580
she has from me.

Creon

            And I, as thirdsman to you,
am rated as the equal of you two?

Oedipus

    Yes, and it's there you've proved yourself false friend.

Creon

Not if you will reflect on it as I do.
Consider, first, if you think any one
would choose to rule and fear rather than rule   585
and sleep untroubled by a fear if power
were equal in both cases. I, at least,
I was not born with such a frantic yearning
to be a king—but to do what kings do.
And so it is with every one who has learned
wisdom and self-control. As it stands now,
the prizes are all mine—and without fear.   590
But if I were the king myself, I must
do much that went against the grain.
How should despotic rule seem sweeter to me
than painless power and an assured authority?
I am not so besotted yet that I
want other honours than those that come with profit.   595
Now every man's my pleasure; every man greets me;
now those who are your suitors fawn on me,—
success for them depends upon my favour.
Why should I let all this go to win that?
My mind would not be traitor if it's wise;   600
I am no treason lover, of my nature,
nor would I ever dare to join a plot.
Prove what I say. Go to the oracle
at Pytho and inquire about the answers,
if they are as I told you. For the rest,   605
if you discover I laid any plot
together with the seer kill me, I say,
not only by your vote but by my own.
But do not charge me on obscure opinion
without some proof to back it. It's not just
lightly to count your knaves as honest men,   610
nor honest men as knaves. To throw away
an honest friend is, as it were, to throw
your life away, which a man loves the best.

In time you will know all with certainty;
time is the only test of honest men,
one day is space enough to know a rogue.

Chorus

His words are wise, king, if one fears to fall.
Those who are quick of temper are not safe.

Oedipus

When he that plots against me secretly
moves quickly, I must quickly counterplot.
If I wait taking no decisive measure   620
his business will be done, and mine be spoiled.

Creon

What do you want to do then? Banish me?

Oedipus

No, certainly; kill you, not banish you.[1]

Creon

I do not think that you've your wits about you.   626

Oedipus

For my own interests, yes.

Creon

                              But for mine, too,
you should think equally.

Oedipus

                              You are a rogue.

Creon

Suppose you do not understand?

Oedipus

                       But yet
I must be ruler.

1. Two lines omitted here owing to the confusion in the dialogue consequent on
the loss of a third line. The lines as they stand in Jebb's edition (1902) are:

Oed.: That you may show what manner of thing is envy.
Creon: You speak as one that will not yield or trust.
[Oed. lost line.]

Creon
> Not if you rule badly.

Oedipus
O, city, city!

Creon
> I too have some share   630
in the city; it is not yours alone.

Chorus
Stop, my lords! Here—and in the nick of time
I see Jocasta coming from the house;
with her help lay the quarrel that now stirs you.

> (*Enter Jocasta.*)

Jocasta
For shame! Why have you raised this foolish squabbling
brawl? Are you not ashamed to air your private   635
griefs when the country's sick? Go in, you, Oedipus,
and you, too, Creon, into the house. Don't magnify
your nothing troubles.

Creon
> Sister, Oedipus,
your husband, thinks he has the right to do
terrible wrongs—he has but to choose between   640
two terrors: banishing or killing me.

Oedipus
He's right, Jocasta; for I find him plotting
with knavish tricks against my person.

Creon
That God may never bless me! May I die
accursed, if I have been guilty of   645
one tittle of the charge you bring against me!

Jocasta
I beg you, Oedipus, trust him in this,
spare him for the sake of this his oath to God,
for my sake, and the sake of those who stand here.

Chorus

Be gracious, be merciful,
we beg of you.   649

Oedipus

In what would you have me yield?

Chorus

He has been no silly child in the past.
He is strong in his oath now.
Spare him.

Oedipus

Do you know what you ask?

Chorus

Yes.

Oedipus

Tell me then.

Chorus

He has been your friend before all men's eyes; do not cast him   656
away dishonoured on an obscure conjecture.

Oedipus

I would have you know that this request of yours
really requests my death or banishment.

Chorus

May the Sun God, king of Gods, forbid! May I die without God's   660
blessing, without friends' help, if I had any such thought. But my
spirit is broken by my unhappiness for my wasting country; and   665
this would but add troubles amongst ourselves to the other
troubles.

Oedipus

Well, let him go then—if I must die ten times for it,   669
or be sent out dishonoured into exile.
It is your lips that prayed for him I pitied,
not his; wherever he is, I shall hate him.

Creon

I see you sulk in yielding and you're dangerous
when you are out of temper; natures like yours
are justly heaviest for themselves to bear.   675

Oedipus

Leave me alone! Take yourself off, I tell you.

Creon

I'll go, you have not known me, but they have,
and they have known my innocence.

(*Exit.*)

Chorus

Won't you take him inside, lady?

Jocasta

Yes, when I've found out what was the matter.   680

Chorus

There was some misconceived suspicion of a story, and on the
other side the sting of injustice.

Jocasta

So, on both sides?

Chorus

Yes.

Jocasta

What was the story?

Chorus

I think it best, in the interests of the country, to leave it where   685
it ended.

Oedipus

You see where you have ended, straight of judgment
although you are, by softening my anger.

Chorus

Sir, I have said before and I say again—be sure that I would have   689
been proved a madman, bankrupt in sane council, if I should put
you away, you who steered the country I love safely when she

was crazed with troubles. God grant that now, too, you may   695
prove a fortunate guide for us.

Jocasta
Tell me, my lord, I beg of you, what was it
that roused your anger so?

Oedipus
                              Yes, I will tell you.   700
I honour you more than I honour them.
It was Creon and the plots he laid against me.

Jocasta
Tell me—if you can clearly tell the quarrel—

Oedipus
                              Creon says
that I'm the murderer of Laius.

Jocasta
Of his own knowledge or on information?

Oedipus
He sent this rascal prophet to me, since   705
he keeps his own mouth clean of any guilt.

Jocasta
Do not concern yourself about this matter;
listen to me and learn that human beings
have no part in the craft of prophecy.
Of that I'll show you a short proof.   710
There was an oracle once that came to Laius,—
I will not say that it was Phoebus' own,
but it was from his servants—and it told him
that it was fate that he should die a victim
at the hands of his own son, a son to be born
of Laius and me. But, see now, he,
the king, was killed by foreign highway robbers   715
at a place where three roads meet—so goes the story;
and for the son—before three days were out
after his birth King Laius pierced his ankles

and by the hands of others cast him forth
upon a pathless hillside. So Apollo   720
failed to fulfill his oracle to the son,
that he should kill his father, and to Laius
also proved false in that the thing he feared,
death at his son's hands, never came to pass.
So clear in this case were the oracles,
so clear and false. Give them no heed, I say;
what God discovers need of, easily
he shows to us himself.   725

Oedipus

                O dear Jocasta,
as I hear this from you, there comes upon me
a wandering of the soul—I could run mad.

Jocasta

What trouble is it, that you turn again
and speak like this?

Oedipus

              I thought I heard you say
that Laius was killed at a crossroads.   730

Jocasta

Yes, that was how the story went and still
that word goes round.

Oedipus

            Where is this place, Jocasta,
where he was murdered?

Jocasta

           Phocis is the country
and the road splits there, one of two roads from Delphi,
another comes from Daulia.

Oedipus

           How long ago is this?   735

Jocasta

The news came to the city just before

you became king and all men's eyes looked to you.
What is it, Oedipus, that's in your mind?

Oedipus

What have you designed, O Zeus, to do with me?

Jocasta

What is the thought that troubles your heart?

Oedipus

Don't ask me yet—tell me of Laius— 740
How did he look? How old or young was he?

Jocasta

He was a tall man and his hair was grizzled
already—nearly white—and in his form
not unlike you.

Oedipus

               O God, I think I have
called curses on myself in ignorance. 745

Jocasta

What do you mean? I am terrified
when I look at you.

Oedipus

               I have a deadly fear
that the old seer had eyes. You'll show me more
if you can tell me one more thing.

Jocasta

                      I will.
I'm frightened,—but if I can understand,
I'll tell you all you ask.

Oedipus

               How was his company? 750
Had he few with him when he went this journey,
or many servants, as would suit a prince?

Jocasta

In all there were but five, and among them
a herald; and one carriage for the king.

Oedipus

It's plain—its plain—who was it told you this?   755

Jocasta

The only servant that escaped safe home.

Oedipus

Is he at home now?

Jocasta

No, when he came home again
and saw you king and Laius was dead,
he came to me and touched my hand and begged   760
that I should send him to the fields to be
my shepherd and so he might see the city
as far off as he might. So I
sent him away. He was an honest man,
as slaves go, and was worthy of far more
than what he asked of me.

Oedipus

O, how I wish that he could come back quickly!   765

Jocasta

He can. Why is your heart so set on this?

Oedipus

O dear Jocasta, I am full of fears
that I have spoken far too much; and therefore
I wish to see this shepherd.

Jocasta

He will come;
but, Oedipus, I think I'm worthy too
to know what it is that disquiets you.   770

Oedipus

It shall not be kept from you, since my mind
has gone so far with its forebodings. Whom
should I confide in rather than you, who is there
of more importance to me who have passed
through such a fortune?

Polybus was my father, king of Corinth,
and Merope, the Dorian, my mother.   775
I was held greatest of the citizens
in Corinth till a curious chance befell me
as I shall tell you—curious, indeed,
but hardly worth the store I set upon it.
There was a dinner and at it a man,
a drunken man, accused me in his drink   780
of being bastard. I was furious
but held my temper under for that day.
Next day I went and taxed my parents with it;
they took the insult very ill from him,
the drunken fellow who had uttered it.
So I was comforted for their part, but   785
still this thing rankled always, for the story
crept about widely. And I went at last
to Pytho, though my parents did not know.
But Phoebus sent me home again unhonoured
in what I came to learn, but he foretold   790
other and desperate horrors to befall me,
that I was fated to lie with my mother,
and show to daylight an accursed breed
which men would not endure, and I was doomed
to be murderer of the father that begot me.
When I heard this I fled, and in the days
that followed I would measure from the stars   795
the whereabouts of Corinth—yes, I fled
to somewhere where I should not see fulfilled
the infamies told in that dreadful oracle.
And as I journeyed I came to the place
where, as you say, this king met with his death.
Jocasta, I will tell you the whole truth.   800
When I was near the branching of the crossroads,
going on foot, I was encountered by
a herald and a carriage with a man in it,
just as you tell me. He that led the way

and the old man himself wanted to thrust me 805
out of the road by force. I became angry
and struck the coachman who was pushing me.
When the old man saw this he watched his moment,
and as I passed he struck me from his carriage,
full on the head with his two pointed goad.
But he was paid in full and presently 810
my stick had struck him backwards from the car
and he rolled out of it. And then I killed them
all. If it happened there was any tie
of kinship twixt this man and Laius,
who is then now more miserable than I, 815
what man on earth so hated by the Gods,
since neither citizen nor foreigner
may welcome me at home or even greet me,
but drive me out of doors? And it is I,
I and no other have so cursed myself. 820
And I pollute the bed of him I killed
by the hands that killed him. Was I not born evil?
Am I not utterly unclean? I had to fly
and in my banishment not even see
my kindred nor set foot in my own country, 825
or otherwise my fate was to be yoked
in marriage with my mother and kill my father,
Polybus who begot me and had reared me.
Would not one rightly judge and say that on me
these things were sent by some malignant God? 830
O no, no, no—O holy majesty
of God on high, may I not see that day!
May I be gone out of men's sight before
I see the deadly taint of this disaster
come upon me.

Chorus

Sir, we too fear these things. But until you see this man face to
face and hear his story, hope. 835

Oedipus

Yes, I have just this much of hope—to wait until the herdsman comes.

Jocasta

And when he comes, what do you want with him?

Oedipus

I'll tell you; if I find that his story is the same as yours, I at least will be clear of this guilt.   840

Jocasta

Why what so particularly did you learn from my story?

Oedipus

You said that he spoke of highway *robbers* who killed Laius. Now if he uses the same number, it was not I who killed him. One man cannot be the same as many. But if he speaks of a man travelling   845 alone, then clearly the burden of the guilt inclines towards me.

Jocasta

Be sure, at least, that this was how he told the story. He cannot unsay it now, for every one in the city heard it—not I alone. But,   850 Oedipus, even if he diverges from what he said then, he shall never prove that the murder of Laius squares rightly with the prophecy—for Loxias declared that the king should be killed by his own son. And that poor creature did not kill him surely,—   855 for he died himself first. So as far as prophecy goes, henceforward I shall not look to the right hand or the left.

Oedipus

Right. But yet, send some one for the peasant to bring him here;   860 do not neglect it.

Jocasta

I will send quickly. Now let me go indoors. I will do nothing except what pleases you.

                                                                          (*Exeunt.*)

Chorus

   Strophe
May destiny ever find me

pious in word and deed   865
prescribed by the laws that live on high:
laws begotten in the clear air of heaven,
whose only father is Olympus;
no mortal nature brought them to birth,
no forgetfulness shall lull them to sleep;   870
for God is great in them and grows not old.

   Antistrophe
Insolence breeds the tyrant, insolence
if it is glutted with a surfeit, unseasonable, unprofitable,   875
climbs to the roof-top and plunges
sheer down to the ruin that must be,
and there its feet are no service.
But I pray that the God may never   880
abolish the eager ambition that profits the state.
For I shall never cease to hold the God as our protector.

   Strophe
If a man walks with haughtiness
of hand or word and gives no heed   885
to Justice and the shrines of Gods
despises—may an evil doom
smite him for his ill-starred pride of heart!—
if he reaps gains without justice
and will not hold from impiety   890
and his fingers itch for untouchable things.
When such things are done, what man shall contrive
to shield his soul from the shafts of the God?
When such deeds are held in honour,   895
why should I honour the Gods in the dance?

   Antistrophe
No longer to the holy place,
to the navel of earth I'll go
to worship, nor to Abae
nor to Olympia,   900
unless the oracles are proved to fit,
for all men's hands to point at.

O Zeus, if you are rightly called
the sovereign lord, all-mastering,
let this not escape you nor your ever-living power!   905
The oracles concerning Laius
are old and dim and men regard them not.
Apollo is nowhere clear in honour; God's service perishes.   910

(*Enter Jocasta, carrying garlands.*)

Jocasta

Princes of the land, I have had the thought to go
to the Gods' temples, bringing in my hand
garlands and gifts of incense, as you see.
For Oedipus excites himself too much
at every sort of trouble, not conjecturing,   915
like a man of sense, what will be from what was,
but he is always at the speaker's mercy,
when he speaks terrors. I can do no good
by my advice, and so I came as suppliant
to you, Lycaean Apollo, who are nearest.
These are the symbols of my prayer and this   920
my prayer: grant us escape free of the curse.
Now when we look to him we are all afraid;
he's pilot of our ship and he is frightened.

(*Enter Messenger.*)

Messenger

Might I learn from you, sirs, where is the house of Oedipus? Or   925
best of all, if you know, where is the king himself?

Chorus

This is his house and he is within doors. This lady is his wife and
mother of his children.

Messenger

God bless you, lady, and God bless your household! God bless   930
Oedipus' noble wife!

Jocasta

God bless you, sir, for your kind greeting! What do you want
of us that you have come here? What have you to tell us?

Messenger

    Good news, lady. Good for your house and for your husband.

Jocasta

    What is your news? Who sent you to us? 935

Messenger

    I come from Corinth and the news I bring will give you pleasure. Perhaps a little pain too.

Jocasta

    What is this news of double meaning?

Messenger

    The people of the Isthmus will choose Oedipus to be their king. 940 That is the rumour there.

Jocasta

    But isn't their king still old Polybus?

Messenger

    No. He is in his grave. Death has got him.

Jocasta

    Is that the truth? Is Oedipus' father dead?

Messenger

    May I die myself if it be otherwise!

Jocasta (to a servant)

    Be quick and run to the King with the news! O oracles of the 945 Gods, where are you now? It was from this man Oedipus fled, lest he should be his murderer! And now he is dead, in the course of nature, and not killed by Oedipus.

                              (Enter Oedipus.)

Oedipus

    Dearest Jocasta, why have you sent for me? 950

Jocasta

    Listen to this man and when you hear reflect what is the outcome of the holy oracles of the Gods.

Oedipus

    Who is he? What is his message for me?

Jocasta

He is from Corinth and he tells us that your father Polybus is   955
dead and gone.

Oedipus

What's this you say, sir? Tell me yourself.

Messenger

Since this is the first matter you want clearly told: Polybus has
gone down to death. You may be sure of it.

Oedipus

By treachery or sickness?   960

Messenger

A small thing will put old bodies asleep.

Oedipus

So he died of sickness, it seems,—poor old man!

Messenger

Yes, and of age—the long years he had measured.

Oedipus

Ha! Ha! O dear Jocasta, why should one
look to the Pythian hearth? Why should one look   965
to the birds screaming overhead? They prophesied
that I should kill my father! But he's dead,
and hidden deep in earth, and I stand here
who never laid a hand on spear against him,—
unless perhaps he died of longing for me,
and thus I am his murderer. But they,   970
the oracles, as they stand—he's taken them
away with him, they're dead as he himself is,
and worthless.

Jocasta

                That I told you before now.

Oedipus

You did, but I was misled by my fear.

Jocasta

Then lay no more of them to heart, not one   975

Oedipus
But surely I must fear my mother's bed?

Jocasta
Why should man fear since chance is all in all
for him, and he can clearly foreknow nothing?
Best to live lightly, as one can, unthinkingly.
As to your mother's marriage bed,—don't fear it.   980
Before this, in dreams too, as well as oracles,
many a man has lain with his own mother.
But he to whom such things are nothing bears
his life most easily.

Oedipus
All that you say would be said perfectly
if she were dead; but since she lives I must   985
still fear, although you talk so well, Jocasta.

Jocasta
Still in your father's death there's light of comfort?

Oedipus
Great light of comfort; but I fear the living.

Messenger
Who is the woman that makes you afraid?

Oedipus
Merope, old man, Polybus' wife.   990

Messenger
What about her frightens the queen and you?

Oedipus
A terrible oracle, stranger, from the Gods.

Messenger
Can it be told? Or does the sacred law
forbid another to have knowledge of it?

Oedipus
O no! Once on a time Loxias said
that I should lie with my own mother and   995

take on my hands the blood of my own father.
And so for these long years I've lived away
from Corinth; it has been to my great happiness;
but yet it's sweet to see the face of parents.

Messenger

This was the fear which drove you out of Corinth?   1000

Oedipus

Old man, I did not wish to kill my father.

Messenger

Why should I not free you from this fear, sir,
since I have come to you in all goodwill?

Oedipus

You would not find me thankless if you did.

Messenger

Why, it was just for this I brought the news,—   1005
to earn your thanks when you had come safe home.

Oedipus

No, I will never come near my parents.

Messenger

                        Son,
it's very plain you don't know what you're doing.

Oedipus

What do you mean, old man? For God's sake, tell me.

Messenger

If your homecoming is checked by fears like these.   1010

Oedipus

Yes, I'm afraid that Phoebus may prove right.

Messenger

The murder and the incest?

Oedipus

                    Yes, old man;
that is my constant terror.

Messenger
                              Do you know
that all your fears are empty?

Oedipus
                              How is that,   1015
if they are father and mother and I their son?

Messenger
  Because Polybus was no kin to you in blood.

Oedipus
  What, was not Polybus my father?

Messenger
  No more than I but just so much.

Oedipus
                              How can
my father be my father as much as one
that's nothing to me?

Messenger
                              Neither he nor I   1020
begat you.

Oedipus
                              Why then did he call me son?

Messenger
  A gift he took you from these hands of mine.

Oedipus
  Did he love so much what he took from another's hand?

Messenger
  His childlessness before persuaded him.

Oedipus
  Was I a child you bought or found when I   1025
was given to him?

Messenger
                              On Cithaeron's slopes
in the twisting thickets you were found.

Oedipus
                              And why
were you a traveller in those parts?

Messenger
                              I was
in charge of mountain flocks.

Oedipus
                              You were a shepherd?
A hireling vagrant?

Messenger
                              Yes, but at least at that time   1030
the man that saved your life, son.

Oedipus
What ailed me when you took me in your arms?

Messenger
In that your ankles should be witnesses.

Oedipus
Why do you speak of that old pain?

Messenger
                              I loosed you;
the tendons of your feet were pierced and fettered,—

Oedipus
My swaddling clothes brought me a rare disgrace.   1035

Messenger
So that from this you're called your present name.

Oedipus
Was this my father's doing or my mother's?
For God's sake, tell me.

Messenger
                              I don't know, but he
who gave you to me has more knowledge than I.

Oedipus
You yourself did not find me then? You took me
from someone else?

Messenger

                    Yes, from another shepherd.   1040

Oedipus

Who was he? Do you know him well enough
to tell?

Messenger

                   He was called Laius' man.

Oedipus

You mean the king who reigned here in the old days?

Messenger

Yes, he was that man's shepherd.

Oedipus

                Is he alive   1045
still, so that I could see him?

Messenger

                You who live here
would know that best.

Oedipus

                Do any of you here
know of this shepherd whom he speaks about
in town or in the fields? Tell me. It's time   1050
that this was found out once for all.

Chorus

I think he is none other than the peasant
whom you have sought to see already; but
Jocasta here can tell us best of that.

Oedipus

Jocasta, do you know about this man
whom we have sent for? Is he the man he mentions?   1055

Jocasta

Why ask of whom he spoke? Don't give it heed;
nor try to keep in mind what has been said.
It will be wasted labour.

Oedipus

                    With such clues
I could not fail to bring my birth to light.

Jocasta

    I beg you—do not hunt this out—I beg you,   1060
if you have any care for your own life.
What I am suffering is enough.

Oedipus

                    Keep up
your heart, Jocasta. Though I'm proved a slave,
thrice slave, and though my mother is thrice slave,
you'll not be shown to be of lowly lineage.

Jocasta

    O be persuaded by me, I entreat you;
do not do this.

Oedipus

    I will not be persuaded to let be   1065
the chance of finding out the whole thing clearly.

Jocasta

    It is because I wish you well that I
give you this counsel—and it's the best counsel.

Oedipus

    Then the best counsel vexes me, and has
for some while since.

Jocasta

                  O Oedipus, God help you!
God keep you from the knowledge of who you are!

Oedipus

    Here, some one, go and fetch the shepherd for me;
and let her find her joy in her rich family!   1070

Jocasta

    O Oedipus, unhappy Oedipus!
that is all I can call you, and the last thing
that I shall ever call you.

                                  (*Exit.*)

Chorus

    Why has the queen gone, Oedipus, in wild
    grief rushing from us? I am afraid that trouble   1075
    will break out of this silence.

Oedipus

    Break out what will! I at least shall be
    willing to see my ancestry, though humble.
    Perhaps she is ashamed of my low birth,
    for she has all a woman's high-flown pride.
    But I account myself a child of Fortune,   1080
    beneficent Fortune, and I shall not be
    dishonoured. She's the mother from whom I spring;
    the months, my brothers, marked me, now as small,
    and now again as mighty. Such is my breeding,
    and I shall never prove so false to it,   1085
    as not to find the secret of my birth.

Chorus

    Strophe

    If I am a prophet and wise of heart
    you shall not fail, Cithaeron,
    by the limitless sky, you shall not!—   1090
    to know at tomorrow's full moon
    that Oedipus honours you,
    as native to him and mother and nurse at once;
    and that you are honoured in dancing by us, as finding favour in
        sight of our king.
    Apollo, to whom we cry, find these things pleasing!

    Antistrophe

    Who was it bore you, child? One of   1098
    the long-lived nymphs who lay with Pan—
    the father who treads the hills?
    Or was she a bride of Loxias, your mother? The grassy slopes
    are all of them dear to him. Or perhaps Cyllene's king   1104
    or the Bacchants' God that lives on the tops

of the hills received you a gift from some
one of the Helicon Nymphs, with whom he mostly plays?

(Enter an old man, led by Oedipus' servants.)

Oedipus

If some one like myself who never met him   1110
may make a guess,—I think this is the herdsman,
whom we were seeking. His old age is consonant
with the other. And besides, the men who bring him
I recognize as my own servants. You   1115
perhaps may better me in knowledge since
you've seen the man before.

Chorus

                You can be sure
I recognize him. For if Laius
had ever an honest shepherd, this was he.

Oedipus

You, sir, from Corinth, I must ask you first,
is this the man you spoke of?   1120

Messenger

             This is he
before your eyes.

Oedipus

             Old man, look here at me
and tell me what I ask you. Were you ever
a servant of King Laius?

Herdsman

             I was,—
no slave he bought but reared in his own house.

Oedipus

What did you do as work? How did you live?

Herdsman

Most of my life was spent among the flocks.   1125

Oedipus

In what part of the country did you live?

Herdsman
  Cithaeron and the places near to it.

Oedipus
  And somewhere there perhaps you knew this man?

Herdsman
  What was his occupation? Who?

Oedipus
                    This man here,   1130
  have you had any dealings with him?

Herdsman
                    No—
  not such that I can quickly call to mind.

Messenger
  That is no wonder, master. But I'll make him remember what he
  does not know. For I know, that he well knows the country of
  Cithaeron, how he with two flocks, I with one kept company for   1135
  three years—each year half a year—from spring till autumn time
  and then when winter came I drove my flocks to our fold home
  again and he to Laius' steadings. Well—am I right or not in what   1140
  I said we did?

Herdsman
  You're right—although it's a long time ago.

Messenger
  Do you remember giving me a child
  to bring up as my foster child?

Herdsman
                    What's this?
  Why do you ask this question?

Messenger
                    Look old man,   1145
  here he is—here's the man who was that child!

Herdsman
  Death take you! Won't you hold your tongue?

Oedipus
> No, no,
do not find fault with him, old man. Your words
are more at fault than his.

Herdsman
> O best of masters,
how do I give offense?

Oedipus
> When you refuse   1150
to speak about the child of whom he asks you.

Herdsman
He speaks out of his ignorance, without meaning.

Oedipus
If you'll not talk to gratify me, you
will talk with pain to urge you.

Herdsman
> O please, sir,
don't hurt an old man, sir.

Oedipus (to the servants)
> Here, one of you,
twist his hands behind him.

Herdsman
> Why, God help me, why?   1155
What do you want to know?

Oedipus
> You gave a child
to him,—the child he asked you of?

Herdsman
> I did.
I wish I'd died the day I did.

Oedipus
> You will
unless you tell me truly.

Herdsman

And I'll die
far worse if I should tell you.

Oedipus

This fellow   1160
is bent on more delays, as it would seem.

Herdsman

O no, no! I have told you that I gave it.

Oedipus

Where did you get this child from? Was it your own or did you
get it from another?

Herdsman

Not
my own at all; I had it from some one.

Oedipus

One of these citizens? or from what house?

Herdsman

O master, please—I beg you, master, please   1165
don't ask me more.

Oedipus

You're a dead man if I
ask you again.

Herdsman

It was one of the children
of Laius.

Oedipus

A slave? Or born in wedlock?

Herdsman

O God, I am on the brink of frightful speech.

Oedipus

And I of frightful hearing. But I must hear.   1170

Herdsman

The child was called his child; but she within,
your wife would tell you best how all this was.

Oedipus
  She gave it to you?

Herdsman
               Yes, she did, my lord.

Oedipus
  To do what with it?

Herdsman
               Make away with it.

Oedipus
  She was so hard—its mother? 1175

Herdsman
               Aye, through fear
  of evil oracles.

Oedipus
               Which?

Herdsman
               They said that he
  should kill his parents.

Oedipus
               How was it that you
  gave it away to this old man?

Herdsman
               O master,
  I pitied it, and thought that I could send it
  off to another country and this man
  was from another country. But he saved it 1180
  for the most terrible troubles. If you are
  the man he says you are, you're bred to misery.

Oedipus
  O, O, O, they will all come,
  all come out clearly! Light of the sun, let me
  look upon you no more after today!
  I who first saw the light bred of a match
  accursed, and accursed in my living
  with them I lived with, cursed in my killing. 1185

               (Exeunt all but the Chorus.)

Chorus
    Strophe
O generations of men, how I
count you as equal with those who live
not at all!
What man, what man on earth wins more   1190
of happiness than a seeming
and after that turning away?
Oedipus, you are my pattern of this,
Oedipus, you and your fate!
Luckless Oedipus, whom of all men
I envy not at all.   1196

    Antistrophe
In as much as he shot his bolt
beyond the others and won the prize
of happiness complete—
O Zeus—and killed and reduced to nought
the hooked taloned maid of the riddling speech,
standing a tower against death for my land:
hence he was called my king and hence
was honoured the highest of all
honours; and hence he ruled
in the great city of Thebes.

    Strophe
But now whose tale is more miserable?   1204
Who is there lives with a savager fate?
Whose troubles so reverse his life as his?

O Oedipus, the famous prince
for whom a great haven
the same both as father and son
sufficed for generation,
how, O how, have the furrows ploughed
by your father endured to bear you, poor wretch,
and hold their peace so long?

Antistrophe
Time who sees all has found you out   1213
against your will; judges your marriage accursed,
begetter and begot at one in it.

O child of Laius,
would I had never seen you.
I weep for you and cry
a dirge of lamentation.

To speak directly, I drew my breath
from you at the first and so now I lull   1222
my mouth to sleep with your name.

                             (Enter a second messenger.)

Second Messenger
O Princes always honoured by our country,
what deeds you'll hear of and what horrors see,
what grief you'll feel, if you as true born Thebans   1225
care for the house of Labdacus's sons.
Phasis nor Ister cannot purge this house,
I think, with all their streams, such things
it hides, such evils shortly will bring forth
into the light, whether they will or not;   1230
and troubles hurt the most
when they prove self-inflicted.

Chorus
What we had known before did not fall short
of bitter groaning's worth; what's more to tell?

Second Messenger
Shortest to hear and tell—our glorious queen   1235
Jocasta's dead.

Chorus
                     Unhappy woman! How?
Second Messenger
By her own hand. The worst of what was done
you cannot know. You did not see the sight.
Yet in so far as I remember it

you'll hear the end of our unlucky queen.   1240
When she came raging into the house she went
straight to her marriage bed, tearing her hair
with both her hands, and crying upon Laius   1245
long dead—Do you remember, Laius,
that night long past which bred a child for us
to send you to your death and leave
a mother making children with her son?
And then she groaned and cursed the bed in which
she brought forth husband by her husband, children   1250
by her own child, an infamous double bond.
How after that she died I do not know,—
for Oedipus distracted us from seeing.
He burst upon us shouting and we looked
to him as he paced frantically around,
begging us always: Give me a sword, I say,   1255
to find this wife no wife, this mother's womb,
this field of double sowing whence I sprang
and where I sowed my children! As he raved
some god showed him the way—none of us there.
Bellowing terribly and led by some   1260
invisible guide he rushed on the two doors,—
wrenching the hollow bolts out of their sockets,
he charged inside. There, there, we saw his wife
hanging, the twisted rope around her neck.
When he saw her, he cried out fearfully   1265
and cut the dangling noose. Then, as she lay,
poor woman, on the ground, what happened after,
was terrible to see. He tore the brooches—
the gold chased brooches fastening her robe—
away from her and lifting them up high
dashed them on his own eyeballs, shrieking out   1270
such things as: they will never see the crime
I have committed or had done upon me!
Dark eyes, now in the days to come look on
forbidden faces, do not recognize

those whom you long for—with such imprecations
he struck his eyes again and yet again   1275
with the brooches. And the bleeding eyeballs gushed
and stained his beard—no sluggish oozing drops
but a black rain and bloody hail poured down.

So it has broken—and not on one head   1280
but troubles mixed for husband and for wife.
The fortune of the days gone by was true
good fortune—but today groans and destruction
and death and shame—of all ills can be named   1285
not one is missing.

Chorus
Is he now in any ease from pain?

Second Messenger
                          He shouts
for some one to unbar the doors and show him
to all the men of Thebes, his father's killer,
his mother's—no I cannot say the word,
it is unholy—for he'll cast himself,
out of the land, he says, and not remain   1290
to bring a curse upon his house, the curse
he called upon it in his proclamation. But
he wants for strength, aye, and some one to guide him;
his sickness is too great to bear. You, too,
will be shown that. The bolts are opening.   1295
Soon you will see a sight to waken pity
even in the horror of it.

                         (Enter the blinded Oedipus.)

Chorus
This is a terrible sight for men to see!
I never found a worse!
Poor wretch, what madness came upon you!   1300
What evil spirit leaped upon your life
to your ill-luck—a leap beyond man's strength!
Indeed I pity you, but I cannot

look at you, though there's much I want to ask
and much to learn and much to see.   1305
I shudder at the sight of you.

Oedipus

O, O,
where am I going? Where is my voice   1310
borne on the wind to and fro?
Spirit, how far have you sprung?

Chorus

To a terrible place whereof men's ears
may not hear, nor their eyes behold it.

Oedipus

Darkness!
Horror of darkness enfolding, resistless, unspeakable visitant sped
    by an ill wind in haste!   1315
madness and stabbing pain and memory
of evil deeds I have done!

Chorus

In such misfortunes it's no wonder
if double weighs the burden of your grief.   1320

Oedipus

My friend,
you are the only one steadfast, the only one that attends on me;
you still stay nursing the blind man.
Your care is not unnoticed. I can know   1325
your voice, although this darkness is my world.

Chorus

Doer of dreadful deeds, how did you dare
so far to do despite to your own eyes?
what spirit urged you to it?

Oedipus

It was Apollo, friends, Apollo,
that brought this bitter bitterness, my sorrows to completion.   1330
But the hand that struck me

was none but my own.
Why should I see
whose vision showed me nothing sweet to see?   1335

Chorus
These things are as you say.

Oedipus
What can I see to love?
What greeting can touch my ears with joy?
Take me away, and haste—to a place out of the way!   1340
Take me away, my friends, the greatly miserable,
the most accursed, whom God too hates   1345
above all men on earth!

Chorus
Unhappy in your mind and your misfortune,
would I had never known you!

Oedipus
Curse on the man who took
the cruel bonds from off my legs, as I lay in the field.   1350
He stole me from death and saved me,
no kindly service.
Had I died then
I would not be so burdensome to friends.   1355

Chorus
I, too, could have wished it had been so.

Oedipus
Then I would not have come
to kill my father and marry my mother infamously.
Now I am godless and child of impurity,   1360
begetter in the same seed that created my wretched self.
If there is any ill worse than ill,   1365
that is the lot of Oedipus.

Chorus
I cannot say your remedy was good;
you would be better dead than blind and living.

Oedipus

What I have done here was best done—don't tell me   1370
otherwise, do not give me further counsel.
I do not know with what eyes I could look
upon my father when I die and go
under the earth, nor yet my wretched mother—
those two to whom I have done things deserving
worse punishment than hanging. Would the sight   1375
of children, bred as mine are, gladden me?
No, not these eyes, never. And my city,
its towers and sacred places of the Gods,
of these I robbed my miserable self   1380
when I commanded all to drive *him* out,
the criminal since proved by God impure
and of the race of Laius.
To this guilt I bore witness against myself—
with what eyes shall I look upon my people?   1385
No. If there were a means to choke the fountain
of hearing I would not have stayed my hand
from locking up my miserable carcase,
seeing and hearing nothing; it is sweet   1390
to keep our thoughts out of the range of hurt.

Cithaeron, why did you receive me? why
having received me did you not kill me straight?
And so I had not shown to men my birth.

O Polybus and Corinth and the house,
the old house that I used to call my father's—   1395
what fairness you were nurse to, and what foulness
festered beneath! Now I am found to be
a sinner and a son of sinners. Crossroads,
and hidden glade, oak and the narrow way
at the crossroads, that drank my father's blood   1400
offered you by my hands, do you remember
still what I did as you looked on, and what
I did when I came here? O marriage, marriage!

you bred me and again when you had bred
bred children of your child and showed to men   1405
brides, wives and mothers and the foulest deeds
that can be in this world of ours.

Come—it's unfit to say what is unfit
to do.—I beg of you in God's name hide me   1410
somewhere outside your country, yes, or kill me,
or throw me into the sea, to be forever
out of your sight. Approach and deign to touch me
for all my wretchedness, and do not fear.
No man but I can bear my evil doom.   1415

Chorus

Here Creon comes in fit time to perform
or give advice in what you ask of us.
Creon is left sole ruler in your stead.

Oedipus

Creon! Creon! What shall I say to him?
How can I justly hope that he will trust me?   1420
In what is past I have been proved towards him
an utter liar.

         (Enter Creon.)

Creon

       Oedipus, I've come
not so that I might laugh at you nor taunt you
with evil of the past. But if you still
are without shame before the face of men
reverence at least the flame that gives all life,   1425
our Lord the Sun, and do not show unveiled
to him pollution such that neither land
nor holy rain nor light of day can welcome.

        (To a servant.)

Be quick and take him in. It is most decent   1430
that only kin should see and hear the troubles
of kin.

Oedipus

            I beg you, since you've torn me from
my dreadful expectations and have come
in a most noble spirit to a man
that has used you vilely—do a thing for me.
I shall speak for your own good, not for my own.

Creon

What do you need that you would ask of me?   1435

Oedipus

Drive me from here with all the speed you can
to where I may not hear a human voice.

Creon

Be sure, I would have done this had not I
wished first of all to learn from the God the course
of action I should follow.

Oedipus

            But his word   1440
has been quite clear to let the parricide,
the sinner, die.

Creon

            Yes, that indeed was said.
But in the present need we had best discover
what we should do.

Oedipus

            And will you ask about
a man so wretched?

Creon

            Now even you will trust   1445
the God.

Oedipus

            So. I command you—and will beseech you—
to her that lies inside that house give burial
as you would have it; she is yours and rightly
you will perform the rites for her. For me—

never let this my father's city have me   1450
living a dweller in it. Leave me live
in the mountains where Cithaeron is, that's called
my mountain, which my mother and my father
while they were living would have made my tomb.
So I may die by their decree who sought
indeed to kill me. Yet I know this much: 1455
no sickness and no other thing will kill me.
I would not have been saved from death if not
for some strange evil fate. Well, let my fate
go where it will.

                    Creon, you need not care   1460
about my sons; they're men and so wherever
they are, they will not lack a livelihood.
But my two girls—so sad and pitiful—
whose table never stood apart from mine,
and everything I touched they always shared—   1465
O Creon, have a thought for them! And most
I wish that you might suffer me to touch them
and sorrow with them.

       (Enter Antigone and Ismene, Oedipus' two daughters.)
O my lord! O true noble Creon! Can I   1470
really be touching them, as when I saw?
What shall I say?
Yes, I can hear them sobbing—my two darlings!
and Creon has had pity and has sent me
what I loved most?
Am I right?   1475

Creon

You're right: it was I gave you this
because I knew from old days how you loved them
as I see now.

Oedipus

                God bless you for it, Creon,
and may God guard you better on your road
than he did me!

O children,   1480

where are you? Come here, come to my hands,
a brother's hands which turned your father's eyes,
those bright eyes you knew once, to what you see,
a father seeing nothing, knowing nothing,
begetting you from his own source of life.   1485
I weep for you—I cannot see your faces—
I weep when I think of the bitterness
there will be in your lives, how you must live
before the world. At what assemblages
of citizens will you make one? to what   1490
gay company will you go and not come home
in tears instead of sharing in the holiday?
And when you're ripe for marriage, who will he be,
the man who'll risk to take such infamy
as shall cling to my children, to bring hurt   1495
on them and those that marry with them? What
curse is not there? "Your father killed his father
and sowed the seed where he had sprung himself
and begot you out of the womb that held him."
These insults you will hear. Then who will marry you?   1500
No one, my children; clearly you are doomed
to waste away in barrenness unmarried.
Son of Menoeceus, since you are all the father
left these two girls, and we, their parents, both   1505
are dead to them—do not allow them wander
like beggars, poor and husbandless.
They are of your own blood.
And do not make them equal with myself
in wretchedness; for you can see them now
so young, so utterly alone, save for you only.
Touch my hand, noble Creon, and say yes.   1510
If you were older, children, and were wiser,
there's much advice I'd give you. But as it is,
let this be what you pray: give me a life

wherever there is opportunity
to live, and better life than was my father's.

Creon
Your tears have had enough of scope; now go within the house.   1515

Oedipus
I must obey, though bitter of heart.

Creon
In season, all is good.

Oedipus
Do you know on what conditions I obey?

Creon
                              You tell me them,
and I shall know them when I hear.

Oedipus
                              That you shall send me out
to live away from Thebes.

Creon
                    That gift you must ask of the God.

Oedipus
But I'm now hated by the Gods.

Creon
                    So quickly you'll obtain your prayer.

Oedipus
You consent then?   1520

Creon
                    What I do not mean, I do not use to say.

Oedipus
Now lead me away from here.

Creon
                    Let go the children, then, and come.

Oedipus
Do not take them from me.

Creon

> Do not seek to be master in everything,
> for the things you mastered did not follow you throughout your
> life.

(As Creon and Oedipus go out.)

Chorus

> You that live in my ancestral Thebes, behold this Oedipus,—
> him who knew the famous riddles and was a man most masterful;   1525
> not a citizen who did not look with envy on his lot—
> see him now and see the breakers of misfortune swallow him!
> Look upon that last day always. Count no mortal happy till
> he has passed the final limit of his life secure from pain.   1530

ANTIGONE

Translated by David Grene

INTRODUCTION

Antigone was probably produced in 442 B.C. Though the part of the saga of Thebes with which it deals is subsequent to the action of *Oedipus the King,* and also *Oedipus at Colonus,* the drama itself was certainly the earliest written of the three, which therefore do not compose a formal trilogy.

Through the conflicts between individuals who always remain sharply characterized is written the eternal conflict between private conscience and public authority. The magnificent choral odes carry the terms of this conflict into images which hold good for any time or place.

TRANSLATOR'S NOTE

The above introduction, somewhat abbreviated, is by Richmond Lattimore. I have written a new translation of the *Antigone,* substituting it for the one by Elizabeth Wyckoff. This is part of revisions I have been making in the series, as the remaining editor, and at the suggestion of the Press.

A comparison of the numbered lines in the Greek text and those of my translation will show some discrepancies. In the *Antigone* I found at times that it was impossible to match the two versions line by line. I have renumbered the lines according to my English translation rather than the original Greek text. I thought that in a class today when the teacher wished to cite a line he or she would more usually want to do that for the students from the English at which the students were looking, rather than from the Greek. I trust this will not lead to too much confusion. The differences tend to be a matter of only a few lines.

Some years ago the Court Theatre asked Wendy Doniger and me to do a new prose version of the *Antigone* for their repertory group. We worked in very close collaboration with the actors. Because the Court Theatre rendering was in prose and all the other plays in the series of *The Complete Greek Tragedies* over-whelmingly in verse, I decided to write this new *Antigone* also in verse. But I owe a great deal to the earlier prose version, which I gladly acknowledge, and to Wendy Doniger's partici-pation in it.

CHARACTERS

Antigone

Ismene

Chorus of Theban Elders

Creon

A Sentry

Haemon

Teiresias

A Messenger

Eurydice

Second Messenger

ANTIGONE

*(The two sisters Antigone and Ismene meet in front of the
palace gates in Thebes.)*

Antigone

Ismene, my dear sister,
whose father was my father, can you think of any
of all the evils that stem from Oedipus
that Zeus does not bring to pass for us, while we yet live?
No pain, no ruin, no shame, and no dishonor
but I have seen it in our mischiefs,
yours and mine.
And now what is the proclamation that they tell of
made lately by the commander, publicly,
to all the people? Do you know it? Have you heard it?   10
Don't you notice when the evils due to enemies
are headed towards those we love?

Ismene

Not a word, Antigone, of those we love,
either sweet or bitter, has come to me since the moment
when we lost our two brothers,
on one day, by their hands dealing mutual death.
Since the Argive army fled in this past night,
I know of nothing further, nothing
of better fortune or of more destruction.

Antigone

I knew it well; that is why I sent for you   20
to come outside the palace gates
to listen to me, privately.

Ismene

What is it? Certainly your words
come of dark thoughts.

Antigone
> Yes, indeed; for those two brothers of ours, in burial
> has not Creon honored the one, dishonored the other?
> Eteocles, they say he has used justly
> with lawful rites and hid him in the earth
> to have his honor among the dead men there.
> But the unhappy corpse of Polyneices   30
> he has proclaimed to all the citizens,
> they say, no man may hide
> in a grave nor mourn in funeral,
> but leave unwept, unburied, a dainty treasure
> for the birds that see him, for their feast's delight.
> That is what, they say, the worthy Creon
> has proclaimed for you and me—for me, I tell you—
> and he comes here to clarify to the unknowing
> his proclamation; he takes it seriously;
> for whoever breaks the edict death is prescribed,   40
> and death by stoning publicly.
> There you have it; soon you will show yourself
> as noble both in your nature and your birth,
> or yourself as base, although of noble parents.

Ismene
> If things are as you say, poor sister, how
> can I better them? how loose or tie the knot?

Antigone
> Decide if you will share the work, the deed.

Ismene
> What kind of danger is there? How far have your thoughts gone?

Antigone
> Here is this hand. Will you help it to lift the dead man?

Ismene
> Would you bury him, when it is forbidden the city?   50

Antigone
> At least he is my brother—and yours, too,
> though you deny him. *I* will not prove false to him.

Ismene

You are so headstrong. Creon has forbidden it.

Antigone

It is not for him to keep me from my own.

Ismene

O God!
Consider, sister, how our father died,
hated and infamous; how he brought to light
his own offenses; how he himself struck out
the sight of his two eyes;
his own hand was their executioner.   60
Then, mother and wife, two names in one, did shame
violently on her life, with twisted cords.
Third, our two brothers, on a single day,
poor wretches, themselves worked out their mutual doom.
Each killed the other, hand against brother's hand.
Now there are only the two of us, left behind,
and see how miserable our end shall be
if in the teeth of law we shall transgress
against the sovereign's decree and power.
You ought to realize we are only women,   70
not meant in nature to fight against men,
and that we are ruled, by those who are stronger,
to obedience in this and even more painful matters.
I do indeed beg those beneath the earth
to give me their forgiveness,
since force constrains me,
that I shall yield in this to the authorities.
Extravagant action is not sensible.

Antigone

I would not urge you now; nor if you wanted
to act would I be glad to have you with me.   80
Be as you choose to be; but for myself
I myself will bury him. It will be good
to die, so doing. I shall lie by his side,

loving him as he loved me; I shall be
a criminal—but a religious one.
The time in which I must please those that are dead
is longer than I must please those of this world.
For there I shall lie forever. You, if you like,
can cast dishonor on what the gods have honored.

Ismene
    I will not put dishonor on them, but   90
    to act in defiance of the citizenry,
    my nature does not give me means for that.

Antigone
    Let that be your excuse. But I will go
    to heap the earth on the grave of my loved brother.

Ismene
    How I fear for you, my poor sister!

Antigone
    Do not fear for me. Make straight your own path to destiny.

Ismene
    At least do not speak of this act to anyone else;
    bury him in secret; I will be silent, too.

Antigone
    Oh, oh, no! shout it out. I will hate you still worse
    for silence—should you not proclaim it,   100
    to everyone.

Ismene
    You have a warm heart for such chilly deeds.

Antigone
    I know I am pleasing those I should please most.

Ismene
    If you can do it. But you are in love
    with the impossible.

Antigone

No. When I can no more, then I will stop.

Ismene

It is better not to hunt the impossible
at all.

Antigone

If you will talk like this I will loathe you,
and you will be adjudged an enemy—   110
justly—by the dead's decision. Let me alone
and my folly with me, to endure this terror.
No suffering of mine will be enough
to make me die ignobly.

Ismene

Well, if you will, go on.
Know this; that though you are wrong to go, your friends
are right to love you.

Chorus

Sun's beam, fairest of all
that ever till now shone
on seven-gated Thebes;   120
O golden eye of day, you shone
coming over Dirce's stream;
You drove in headlong rout
the whiteshielded man from Argos,
complete in arms;
his bits rang sharper
under your urging.

Polyneices brought him here
against our land, Polyneices,
roused by contentious quarrel;   130
like an eagle he flew into our country,
with many men-at-arms,
with many a helmet crowned with horsehair.

He stood above the halls, gaping with murderous lances,
encompassing the city's
seven-gated mouth.
But before his jaws would be sated
with our blood, before the fire,
pine fed, should capture our crown of towers,
he went hence—   140
such clamor of war stretched behind his back,
from his dragon foe, a thing he could not overcome.

For Zeus, who hates the most
the boasts of a great tongue,
saw them coming in a great tide,
insolent in the clang of golden armor.
The god struck him down with hurled fire,
as he strove to raise the victory cry,
now at the very winning post.

The earth rose to strike him as he fell swinging.   150
In his frantic onslaught, possessed, he breathed upon us
with blasting winds of hate.
Sometimes the great god of war was on one side,
and sometimes he struck a staggering blow on the other;
the god was a very wheel horse on the right trace.

At seven gates stood seven captains,
ranged equals against equals, and there left
their brazen suits of armor
to Zeus, the god of trophies.
Only those two wretches born of one father and mother   160
set their spears to win a victory on both sides;
they worked out their share in a common death.

Now Victory, whose name is great, has come
to Thebes of many chariots
with joy to answer her joy,
to bring forgetfulness of these wars;
let us go to all the shrines of the gods

and dance all night long.
Let Bacchus lead the dance,
shaking Thebes to trembling.   170

But here is the king of our land,
Creon, son of Menoeceus;
in our new contingencies with the gods,
he is our new ruler.
He comes to set in motion some design—
what design is it? Because he has proposed
the convocation of the elders.
He sent a public summons for our discussion.

Creon
Gentlemen: as for our city's fortune,
the gods have shaken her, when the great waves broke,   180
but the gods have brought her through again to safety.
For yourselves, I chose you out of all and summoned you
to come to me, partly because I knew you
as always loyal to the throne—at first,
when Laïus was king, and then again
when Oedipus saved our city and then again
when he died and you remained with steadfast truth
to their descendants,
until they met their double fate upon one day,
striking and stricken, defiled each by a brother's murder.   190
Now here I am, holding all authority
and the throne, in virtue of kinship with the dead.

It is impossible to know any man—
I mean his soul, intelligence, and judgment—
until he shows his skill in rule and law.
I think that a man supreme ruler of a whole city,
if he does not reach for the best counsel for her,
but through some fear, keeps his tongue under lock and key,   200
him I judge the worst of any;
I have always judged so; and anyone thinking
another man more a friend than his own country,

I rate him nowhere. For my part, God is my witness,
who sees all, always, I would not be silent
if I saw ruin, not safety, on the way
towards my fellow citizens. I would not count
any enemy of my country as a friend—
because of what I know, that she it is
which gives us our security. If she sails upright
and we sail on her, friends will be ours for the making.
In the light of rules like these, I will make her greater still.   210

In consonance with this, I here proclaim
to the citizens about Oedipus' sons.
For Eteocles, who died this city's champion,
showing his valor's supremacy everywhere,
he shall be buried in his grave with every rite
of sanctity given to heroes under earth.
However, his brother, Polyneices, a returned exile,
who sought to burn with fire from top to bottom
his native city, and the gods of his own people;
who sought to taste the blood he shared with us,   220
and lead the rest of us to slavery—
I here proclaim to the city that this man
shall no one honor with a grave and none shall mourn.
You shall leave him without burial; you shall watch him
chewed up by birds and dogs and violated.
Such is my mind in the matter; never by me
shall the wicked man have precedence in honor
over the just. But he that is loyal to the state
in death, in life alike, shall have my honor.

Chorus
    Son of Menoeceus, so it is your pleasure   230
    to deal with foe and friend of this our city.
    To use any legal means lies in your power,
    both about the dead and those of us who live.

Creon
    I understand, then, you will do my bidding.

Chorus
  Please lay this burden on some younger man.

Creon
  Oh, watchers of the corpse I have already.

Chorus
  What else, then, do your commands entail?

Creon
  That you should not side with those who disagree.

Chorus
  There is none so foolish as to love his own death.

Creon
  Yes, indeed those are the wages, but often greed   240
  has with its hopes brought men to ruin.

[*The sentry whose speeches follow represents a remarkable experiment in Greek tragedy in the direction of naturalism of speech. He speaks with marked clumsiness, partly because he is excited and talks almost colloquially. But also the royal presence makes him think apparently that he should be rather grand in his show of respect. He uses odd bits of archaism or somewhat stale poetical passages, particularly in catch phrases. He sounds something like lower-level Shakespearean characters, e.g. Constable Elbow, with his uncertainty about benefactor and malefactor.*]

Sentry
  My lord, I will never claim my shortness of breath
  is due to hurrying, nor were there wings in my feet.
  I stopped at many a lay-by in my thinking;
  I circled myself till I met myself coming back.
  My soul accosted me with different speeches.
  "Poor fool, yourself, why are you going somewhere
  when once you get there you will pay the piper?"
  "Well, aren't you the daring fellow! stopping again?
  and suppose Creon hears the news from someone else—   250

don't you realize that you will smart for that?"
I turned the whole matter over. I suppose I may say
"I made haste slowly" and the short road became long.
However, at last I came to a resolve:
I must go to you; even if what I say
is nothing, really, still I shall say it.
I come here, a man with a firm clutch on the hope
that nothing can betide him save what is fated.

Creon
What is it then that makes you so afraid?

Sentry
No, I want first of all to tell you my side of it.   260
I didn't do the thing; I never saw who did it.
It would not be fair for me to get into trouble.

Creon
You hedge, and barricade the thing itself.
Clearly you have some ugly news for me.

Sentry
Well, you know how disasters make a man
hesitate to be their messenger.

Creon
For God's sake, tell me and get out of here!

Sentry
Yes, I *will* tell you. Someone just now
buried the corpse and vanished. He scattered on the skin
some thirsty dust; he did the ritual,   270
duly, to purge the body of desecration.

Creon
What! Now who on earth could have done that?

Sentry
I do not know. For there was there no mark
of axe's stroke nor casting up of earth
of any mattock; the ground was hard and dry,

unbroken; there were no signs of wagon wheels.
The doer of the deed had left no trace.
But when the first sentry of the day pointed it out,
there was for all of us a disagreeable
wonder. For the body had disappeared;   280
not in a grave, of course; but there lay upon him
a little dust as of a hand avoiding
the curse of violating the dead body's sanctity.
There were no signs of any beast nor dog
that came there; he had clearly not been torn.
There was a tide of bad words at one another,
guard taunting guard, and it might well have ended
in blows, for there was no one there to stop it.
Each one of us was the criminal but no one
manifestly so; all denied knowledge of it.   290
We were ready to take hot bars in our hands
or walk through fire, and call on the gods with oaths
that we had neither done it nor were privy
to a plot with anyone, neither in planning
nor yet in execution.
At last when nothing came of all our searching,
there was one man who spoke, made every head
bow to the ground in fear. For we could not
either contradict him nor yet could we see how
if we did what he said we would come out all right.   300
His word was that we must lay information
about this matter to yourself; we could not cover it.
This view prevailed and the lot of the draw chose me,
unlucky me, to win that prize. So here
I am. I did not want to come,
and you don't want to have me. I know that.
For no one likes the messenger of bad news.

Chorus
　　My lord: I wonder, could this be God's doing?
　　This is the thought that keeps on haunting me.

Creon

    Stop, before your words fill even me with rage,   310
that you should be exposed as a fool, and you so old.
For what you say is surely insupportable
when you say the gods took forethought for this corpse.
Is it out of excess of honor for the man,
for the favors that he did them, they should cover him?
This man who came to burn their pillared temples,
their dedicated offerings—and this land
and laws he would have scattered to the winds?
Or do you see the gods as honoring
criminals? This is not so. But what I am doing   320
now, and other things before this, some men disliked,
within this very city, and muttered against me,
secretly shaking their heads; they would not bow
justly beneath the yoke to submit to me.
I am very sure that these men hired others
to do this thing. I tell you the worse currency
that ever grew among mankind is money. This
sacks cities, this drives people from their homes,
this teaches and corrupts the minds of the loyal
to acts of shame. This displays   330
all kinds of evil for the use of men,
instructs in the knowledge of every impious act.
Those that have done this deed have been paid to do it,
but in the end they will pay for what they have done.

    It is as sure as I still reverence Zeus—
know this right well—and I speak under oath—
if you and your fellows do not find this man
who with his own hand did the burial
and bring him here before me face to face,
your death alone will not be enough for me.   340
You will hang alive till you open up this outrage.
That will teach you in the days to come from what
you may draw profit—safely—from your plundering.

It's not from anything and everything
you can grow rich. You will find out
that ill-gotten gains ruin more than they save.

Sentry

Have I your leave to say something—or should I
just turn and go?

Creon

Don't you know your talk is painful enough already?

Sentry

Is the ache in your ears or in your mind?   350

Creon

Why do you dissect the whereabouts of my pain?

Sentry

Because it is he who did the deed who hurts
your mind. I only hurt your ears that listen.

Creon

I am sure you have been a chatterbox since you were born.

Sentry

All the same, I did not do this thing.

Creon

You might have done this, too, if you sold your soul.

Sentry

It's a bad thing if one judges and judges wrongly.

Creon

You may talk as wittily as you like of judgment.
Only, if you don't bring to light those men
who have done this, you will yet come to say   360
that your wretched gains have brought bad consequences.

Sentry (aside)

It were best that he were found, but whether
the criminal is taken or he isn't—
for that chance will decide—one thing is certain,

you'll never see me coming here again.
I never hoped to escape, never thought I could.
But now I have come off safe, I thank God heartily.

Chorus

Many are the wonders, none
is more wonderful than what is man.
This it is that crosses the sea   370
with the south winds storming and the waves swelling,
breaking around him in roaring surf.
He it is again who wears away
the Earth, oldest of gods, immortal, unwearied,
as the ploughs wind across her from year to year
when he works her with the breed that comes from horses.

The tribe of the lighthearted birds he snares
and takes prisoner the races of savage beasts
and the brood of the fish of the sea,
with the close-spun web of nets.   380
A cunning fellow is man. His contrivances
make him master of beasts of the field
and those that move in the mountains.
So he brings the horse with the shaggy neck
to bend underneath the yoke;
and also the untamed mountain bull;
and speech and windswift thought
and the tempers that go with city living
he has taught himself, and how to avoid
the sharp frost, when lodging is cold   390
under the open sky
and pelting strokes of the rain.
He has a way against everything,
and he faces nothing that is to come
without contrivance.
Only against death
can he call on no means of escape;
but escape from hopeless diseases

he has found in the depths of his mind.
With some sort of cunning, inventive   400
beyond all expectation
he reaches sometimes evil,
and sometimes good.

If he honors the laws of earth,
and the justice of the gods he has confirmed by oath,
high is his city; no city
has he with whom dwells dishonor
prompted by recklessness.
He who is so, may he never
share my hearth!   410
may he never think my thoughts!

Is this a portent sent by God?
I cannot tell.
I know her. How can I say
that this is not Antigone?
Unhappy girl, child of unhappy Oedipus,
what is this?
Surely it is not you they bring here
as disobedient to the royal edict,
surely not you, taken in such folly.   420

Sentry
She is the one who did the deed;
we took her burying him. But where is Creon?

Chorus
He is just coming from the house, when you most need him.

Creon
What is this? What has happened that I come
so opportunely?

Sentry
My lord, there is nothing
that a man should swear he would never do.

Second thoughts make liars of the first resolution.
I would have vowed it would be long enough
before I came again, lashed hence by your threats.   430
But since the joy that comes past hope, and against all hope,
is like no other pleasure in extent,
I have come here, though I break my oath in coming.
I bring this girl here who has been captured
giving the grace of burial to the dead man.
This time no lot chose me; this was my jackpot,
and no one else's. Now, my lord, take her
and as you please judge her and test her; I
am justly free and clear of all this trouble.

Creon

This girl—how did you take her and from where?   440

Sentry

She was burying the man. Now you know all.

Creon

Do you know what you are saying? Do you mean it?

Sentry

She is the one; I saw her burying
the dead man you forbade the burial of.
Now, do I speak plainly and clearly enough?

Creon

How was she seen? How was she caught in the act?

Sentry

This is how it was. When we came there,
with those dreadful threats of yours upon us,
we brushed off all the dust that lay upon
the dead man's body, heedfully   450
leaving it moist and naked.
We sat on the brow of the hill, to windward,
that we might shun the smell of the corpse upon us.

Each of us wakefully urged his fellow
with torrents of abuse, not to be careless
in this work of ours. So it went on,
until in the midst of the sky the sun's bright circle
stood still; the heat was burning. Suddenly
a squall lifted out of the earth a storm of dust,
a trouble in the sky. It filled the plain,   460
ruining all the foliage of the wood
that was around it. The great empty air
was filled with it. We closed our eyes, enduring
this plague sent by the gods. When at long last
we were quit of it, why, then we saw the girl.

She was crying out with the shrill cry
of an embittered bird
that sees its nest robbed of its nestlings
and the bed empty. So, too, when she saw
the body stripped of its cover, she burst out in groans,   470
calling terrible curses on those that had done that deed;
and with her hands immediately
brought thirsty dust to the body; from a shapely brazen
urn, held high over it, poured a triple stream
of funeral offerings; and crowned the corpse.
When we saw that, we rushed upon her and
caught our quarry then and there, not a bit disturbed.
We charged her with what she had done, then and the first time.
She did not deny a word of it—to my joy,
but to my pain as well. It is most pleasant   480
to have escaped oneself out of such troubles
but painful to bring into it those whom we love.
However, it is but natural for me
to count all this less than my own escape.

Creon
  You there, that turn your eyes upon the ground,
  do you confess or deny what you have done?

Antigone
   Yes, I confess; I will not deny my deed.

Creon (to the Sentry)
   You take yourself off where you like.
   You are free of a heavy charge.
   Now, Antigone, tell me shortly and to the point,   490
   did you know the proclamation against your action?

Antigone
   I knew it; of course I did. For it was public.

Creon
   And did you dare to disobey that law?

Antigone
   Yes, it was not Zeus that made the proclamation;
   nor did Justice, which lives with those below, enact
   such laws as that, for mankind. I did not believe
   your proclamation had such power to enable
   one who will someday die to override
   God's ordinances, unwritten and secure.
   They are not of today and yesterday;   500
   they live forever; none knows when first they were.
   These are the laws whose penalties I would not
   incur from the gods, through fear of any man's temper.

   I know that I will die—of course I do—
   even if you had not doomed me by proclamation.
   If I shall die before my time, I count that
   a profit. How can such as I, that live
   among such troubles, not find a profit in death?
   So for such as me, to face such a fate as this
   is pain that does not count. But if I dared to leave   510
   the dead man, my mother's son, dead and unburied,
   that would have been real pain. The other is not.
   Now, if you think me a fool to act like this,
   perhaps it is a fool that judges so.

Chorus

  The savage spirit of a savage father
  shows itself in this girl. She does not know
  how to yield to trouble.

Creon

  I would have you know the most fanatic spirits
  fall most of all. It is the toughest iron,
  baked in the fire to hardness, you may see   520
  most shattered, twisted, shivered to fragments.
  I know hot horses are restrained
  by a small curb. For he that is his neighbor's slave cannot
  be high in spirit. This girl had learned her insolence
  before this, when she broke the established laws.
  But here is still another insolence
  in that she boasts of it, laughs at what she did.
  I swear I am no man and she the man
  if she can win this and not pay for it.
  No; though she were my sister's child or closer   530
  in blood than all that my hearth god acknowledges
  as mine, neither she nor her sister should escape
  the utmost sentence—death. For indeed I accuse her,
  the sister, equally of plotting the burial.
  Summon her. I saw her inside, just now,
  crazy, distraught. When people plot
  mischief in the dark, it is the mind which first
  is convicted of deceit. But surely I hate indeed
  the one that is caught in evil and then makes
  that evil look like good.   540

Antigone

  Do you want anything
  beyond my taking and my execution?

Creon

  Oh, nothing! Once I have that I have everything.

Antigone

   Why do you wait, then? Nothing that you say
   pleases me; God forbid it ever should.
   So my words, too, naturally offend you.
   Yet how could I win a greater share of glory
   than putting my own brother in his grave?
   All that are here would surely say that's true,
   if fear did not lock their tongues up. A prince's power   550
   is blessed in many things, not least in this,
   that he can say and do whatever he likes.

Creon

   You are alone among the people of Thebes
   to see things in that way.

Antigone

   No, these do, too,
   but keep their mouths shut for the fear of you.

Creon

   Are you not ashamed to think so differently
   from them?

Antigone

   There is nothing shameful in honoring my brother.

Creon

   Was not he that died on the other side your brother?   560

Antigone

   Yes, indeed, of my own blood from father and mother.

Creon

   Why then do you show a grace that must be impious
   in *his* sight?

Antigone

   That other dead man
   would never bear you witness in what you say.

Creon
Yes he would, if you put him only on equality
with one that was a desecrator.

Antigone
It was his brother, not his slave, that died.

Creon
He died destroying the country the other defended.

Antigone
The god of death demands these rites for both.   570

Creon
But the good man does not seek an *equal* share only,
with the bad.

Antigone
                        Who knows
if in that other world this is true piety?

Creon
My enemy is still my enemy, even in death.

Antigone
My nature is to join in love, not hate.

Creon
Go then to the world below, yourself, if you
must love. Love *them*. When I am alive no woman shall rule.

Chorus
Here before the gates comes Ismene
shedding tears for the love of a brother.   580
A cloud over her brow casts shame
on her flushed face, as the tears wet
her fair cheeks.

Creon
You there, who lurked in my house, viper-like—
secretly drawing its lifeblood; I never thought

that I was raising two sources of destruction,
two rebels against my throne. Come tell me now,
will you, too, say you bore a hand in the burial
or will you swear that you know nothing of it?

Ismene

  I did it, yes—if she will say I did it   590
  I bear my share in it, bear the guilt, too.

Antigone

  Justice will not allow you what you refused
  and I will have none of your partnership.

Ismene

  But in your troubles I am not ashamed
  to sail with you the sea of suffering.

Antigone

  Where the act was death, the dead are witnesses.
  I do not love a friend who loves in words.

Ismene

  Sister, do not dishonor me, denying me
  a common death with you, a common honoring
  of the dead man.   600

Antigone

  Don't die with me, nor make your own
  what you have never touched. I that die am enough.

Ismene

  What life is there for me, once I have lost you?

Antigone

  Ask Creon; all your care was on his behalf.

Ismene

  Why do you hurt me, when you gain nothing by it?

Antigone

  I am hurt by my own mockery—if I mock you.

Ismene
Even now—what can I do to help you still?

Antigone
Save yourself; I do not grudge you your escape.

Ismene
I cannot bear it! Not even to share your death!

Antigone
Life was your choice, and death was mine.   610

Ismene
You cannot say I accepted that choice in silence.

Antigone
You were right in the eyes of one party, I in the other.

Ismene
Well then, the fault is equally between us.

Antigone
Take heart; you are alive, but my life died
long ago, to serve the dead.

Creon
Here are two girls; I think that one of them
has suddenly lost her wits—the other was always so.

Ismene
Yes, for, my lord, the wits that they are born with
do not stay firm for the unfortunate.
They go astray.   620

Creon
                    Certainly yours do,
when you share troubles with the troublemaker.

Ismene
What life can be mine alone without her?

Creon
                                        Do not
speak of *her*. *She* isn't, anymore.

Ismene
Will you kill your son's wife to be?

Creon
Yes, there are other fields for him to plough.

Ismene
Not with the mutual love of him and her.

Creon
I hate a bad wife for a son of mine.

Antigone
Dear Haemon, how your father dishonors you.   630

Creon
There is too much of you—and of your marriage!

Chorus
Will you rob your son of this girl?

Creon
Death—it is death that will stop the marriage for me.

Chorus
Your decision it seems is taken: she shall die.

Creon
Both you and I have decided it. No more delay.

(He turns to the servants.)

Bring her inside, you. From this time forth,
these must be women, and not free to roam.
For even the stout of heart shrink when they see
the approach of death close to their lives.

Chorus
            Lucky are those whose lives   640
            know no taste of sorrow.
            But for those whose house has been shaken by God
            there is never cessation of ruin;
            it steals on generation after generation

within a breed. Even as the swell
is driven over the dark deep
by the fierce Thracian winds
I see the ancient evils of Labdacus' house
are heaped on the evils of the dead.
No generation frees another, some god   650
strikes them down; there is no deliverance.
Here was the light of hope stretched
over the last roots of Oedipus' house,
and the bloody dust due to the gods below
has mowed it down—that and the folly of speech
and ruin's enchantment of the mind.

Your power, O Zeus, what sin of man can limit?
All-aging sleep does not overtake it,
nor the unwearied months of the gods; and you,
for whom time brings no age,   660
you hold the glowing brightness of Olympus.

For the future near and far,
and the past, this law holds good:
nothing very great
comes to the life of mortal man
without ruin to accompany it.
For Hope, widely wandering, comes to many of mankind
as a blessing,
but to many as the deceiver,
using light-minded lusts;   670
she comes to him that knows nothing
till he burns his foot in the glowing fire.
With wisdom has someone declared
a word of distinction:
that evil seems good to one whose mind
the god leads to ruin,
and but for the briefest moment of time
is his life outside of calamity.

Here is Haemon, youngest of your sons.
Does he come grieving   680
for the fate of his bride to be,
in agony at being cheated of his marriage?

Creon

Soon we will know that better than the prophets.
My son, can it be that you have not heard
of my final decision on your betrothed?
Can you have come here in your fury against your father?
Or have I your love still, no matter what I do?

Haemon

Father, I am yours; with your excellent judgment
you lay the right before me, and I shall follow it.
No marriage will ever be so valued by me   690
as to override the goodness of your leadership.

Creon

Yes, my son, this should always be
in your very heart, that everything else
shall be second to your father's decision.
It is for this that fathers pray to have
obedient sons begotten in their halls,
that they may requite with ill their father's enemy
and honor his friend no less than he would himself.
If a man have sons that are no use to him,
what can one say of him but that he has bred   700
so many sorrows to himself, laughter to his enemies?
Do not, my son, banish your good sense
through pleasure in a woman, since you know
that the embrace grows cold
when an evil woman shares your bed and home.
What greater wound can there be than a false friend?
No. Spit on her, throw her out like an enemy,
this girl, to marry someone in Death's house.
I caught her openly in disobedience
alone out of all this city and I shall not make   710

myself a liar in the city's sight. No, I will kill her.
So let her cry if she will on the Zeus of kinship;
for if I rear those of my race and breeding
to be rebels, surely I will do so with those outside it.
For he who is in his household a good man
will be found a just man, too, in the city.
But he that breaches the law or does it violence
or thinks to dictate to those who govern him
shall never have my good word.
The man the city sets up in authority   720
must be obeyed in small things and in just
but also in their opposites.
I am confident such a man of whom I speak
will be a good ruler, and willing to be well ruled.
He will stand on his country's side, faithful and just,
in the storm of battle. There is nothing worse
than disobedience to authority.
It destroys cities, it demolishes homes;
it breaks and routs one's allies. Of successful lives
the most of them are saved by discipline.   730
So we must stand on the side of what is orderly;
we cannot give victory to a woman.
If we must accept defeat, let it be from a man;
we must not let people say that a woman beat us.

Chorus
    We think, if we are not victims of Time the Thief,
    that you speak intelligently of what you speak.

Haemon
    Father, the natural sense that the gods breed
    in men is surely the best of their possessions.
    I certainly could not declare you wrong—
    may I never know how to do so!—Still there might   740
    be something useful that some other than you might think.
    It is natural for me to be watchful on your behalf
    concerning what all men say or do or find to blame.

Your face is terrible to a simple citizen;
it frightens him from words you dislike to hear.
But what *I* can hear, in the dark, are things like these:
the city mourns for this girl; they think she is dying
most wrongly and most undeservedly
of all womenkind, for the most glorious acts.
Here is one who would not leave her brother unburied,   750
a brother who had fallen in bloody conflict,
to meet his end by greedy dogs or by
the bird that chanced that way. Surely what she merits
is golden honor, isn't it? That's the dark rumor
that spreads in secret. Nothing I own
I value more highly, father, than your success.
What greater distinction can a son have than the glory
of a successful father, and for a father
the distinction of successful children?
Do not bear this single habit of mind, to think   760
that what you say and nothing else is true.
A man who thinks that he alone is right,
or what he says, or what he *is* himself,
unique, such men, when opened up, are seen
to be quite empty. For a man, though he be wise,
it is no shame to learn—learn many things,
and not maintain his views too rigidly.
You notice how by streams in wintertime
the trees that yield preserve their branches safely,
but those that fight the tempest perish utterly.   770
The man who keeps the sheet of his sail tight
and never slackens capsizes his boat
and makes the rest of his trip keel uppermost.
Yield something of your anger, give way a little.
If a much younger man, like me, may have
a judgment, I would say it were far better
to be one altogether wise by nature, but,
as things incline not to be so, then it is good
also to learn from those who advise well.

Chorus

My lord, if he says anything to the point,   780
you should learn from him, and you, too, Haemon,
learn from your father. Both of you
have spoken well.

Creon

Should we that are my age learn wisdom
from young men such as he is?

Haemon

Not learn injustice, certainly. If I am young,
do not look at my years but what I do.

Creon

Is what you do to have respect for rebels?

Haemon

I
would not urge you to be scrupulous   790
towards the wicked.

Creon

Is *she* not tainted by the disease of wickedness?

Haemon

The entire people of Thebes says no to that.

Creon

Should the city tell me how I am to rule them?

Haemon

Do you see what a young man's words these are of yours?

Creon

Must I rule the land by someone else's judgment
rather than my own?

Haemon

There is no city
possessed by one man only.

Creon

Is not the city thought to be the ruler's?   800

Haemon

You would be a fine dictator of a desert.

Creon

It seems this boy is on the woman's side.

Haemon

If you are a woman—my care is all for you.

Creon

You villain, to bandy words with your own father!

Haemon

I see your acts as mistaken and unjust.

Creon

Am I mistaken, reverencing my own office?

Haemon

There is no reverence in trampling on God's honor.

Creon

Your nature is vile, in yielding to a woman.

Haemon

You will not find me yield to what is shameful.

Creon

At least, your argument is all for her.   810

Haemon

Yes, and for you and me—and for the gods below.

Creon

You will never marry her while her life lasts.

Haemon

Then she must die—and dying destroy another.

Creon

Has your daring gone so far, to threaten me?

Haemon

What threat is it to speak against empty judgments?

Creon

 Empty of sense yourself, you will regret
 your schooling of me in sense.

Haemon

          If you were not
 my father, I would say you are insane.

Creon

 You woman's slave, do not try to wheedle me.   820

Haemon

 You want to talk but never to hear and listen.

Creon

 Is that so? By the heavens above you will not—
 be sure of that—get off scot-free, insulting,
 abusing me.

          (He speaks to the servants.)

    You people bring out this creature,
 this hated creature, that she may die before
 his very eyes, right now, next her would-be husband.

Haemon

 Not at my side! Never think that! She will not
 die by my side. But you will never again
 set eyes upon my face. Go then and rage   830
 with such of your friends as are willing to endure it.

Chorus

 The man is gone, my lord, quick in his anger.
 A young man's mind is fierce when he is hurt.

Creon

 Let him go, and do and think things superhuman.
 But these two girls he shall not save from death.

Chorus

 Both of them? Do you mean to kill them both?

Creon

    No, not the one that didn't do anything.
    You are quite right there.

Chorus

    And by what form of death do you mean to kill her?

Creon

    I will bring her where the path is loneliest,   840
    and hide her alive in a rocky cavern there.
    I'll give just enough of food as shall suffice
    for a bare expiation, that the city may avoid pollution.
    In that place she shall call on Hades, god of death,
    in her prayers. That god only she reveres.
    Perhaps she will win from him escape from death
    or at least in that last moment will recognize
    her honoring of the dead is labor lost.

Chorus

    Love undefeated in the fight,
    Love that makes havoc of possessions,   850
    Love who lives at night in a young girl's soft cheeks,
    Who travels over sea, or in huts in the countryside—
    there is no god able to escape you
    nor anyone of men, whose life is a day only,
    and whom you possess is mad.

    You wrench the minds of just men to injustice,
    to their disgrace; this conflict among kinsmen
    it is you who stirred to turmoil.
    The winner is desire. She gleaming kindles
    from the eyes of the girl good to bed.   860
    Love shares the throne with the great powers that rule.
    For the golden Aphrodite holds her play there
    and then no one can overcome her.

    Here I too am borne out of the course of lawfulness
    when I see these things, and I cannot control
    the springs of my tears

when I see Antigone making her way
to her bed—but the bed
that is rest for everyone.

Antigone

You see me, you people of my country,   870
as I set out on my last road of all,
looking for the last time on this light of this sun—
never again. I am alive but Hades who gives sleep to everyone
is leading me to the shores of Acheron,
though I have known nothing of marriage songs
nor the chant that brings the bride to bed.
My husband is to be the Lord of Death.

Chorus

Yes, you go to the place where the dead are hidden,
but you go with distinction and praise.
You have not been stricken by wasting sickness;   880
you have not earned the wages of the sword;
it was your own choice and alone among mankind
you will descend, alive,
to that world of death.

Antigone

But indeed I have heard of the saddest of deaths—
of the Phrygian stranger, daughter of Tantalus,
whom the rocky growth subdued, like clinging ivy.
The rains never leave her, the snow never fails,
as she wastes away. That is how men tell the story.
From streaming eyes her tears wet the crags;   890
most like to her the god brings me to rest.

Chorus

Yes, but she was a god, and god born,
and you are mortal and mortal born.
Surely it is great renown
for a woman that dies, that in life and death
her lot is a lot shared with demigods.

Antigone

You mock me. In the name of our fathers' gods
why do you not wait till I am gone to insult me?
Must you do it face to face?
My city! Rich citizens of my city!   900
You springs of Dirce, you holy groves of Thebes,
famed for its chariots! I would still have you as my witnesses,
with what dry-eyed friends, under what laws
I make my way to my prison sealed like a tomb.
Pity me. Neither among the living nor the dead
do I have a home in common—
neither with the living nor the dead.

Chorus

You went to the extreme of daring
and against the high throne of Justice
you fell, my daughter, grievously.   910
But perhaps it was for some ordeal of your father
that you are paying requital.

Antigone

You have touched the most painful of my cares—
the pity for my father, ever reawakened,
and the fate of all of our race, the famous Labdacids;
the doomed self-destruction of my mother's bed
when she slept with her own son,
my father.
What parents I was born of, God help me!
To them I am going to share their home,   920
the curse on me, too, and unmarried.
Brother, it was a luckless marriage you made,
and dying killed my life.

Chorus

There *is* a certain reverence for piety.
But for him in authority,
he cannot see that authority defied;

it is your own self-willed temper
that has destroyed you.

Antigone
    No tears for me, no friends, no marriage. Brokenhearted
    I am led along the road ready before me.   930
    I shall never again be suffered
    to look on the holy eye of the day.
    But my fate claims no tears—
    no friend cries for me.

Creon (to the servants)
    Don't you know that weeping and wailing before death
    would never stop if one is allowed to weep and wail?
    Lead her away at once. Enfold her
    in that rocky tomb of hers—as I told you to.
    There leave her alone, solitary,
    to die if she so wishes   940
    or live a buried life in such a home;
    we are guiltless in respect of her, this girl.
    But living above, among the rest of us, this life
    she shall certainly lose.

Antigone
    Tomb, bridal chamber, prison forever
    dug in rock, it is to you I am going
    to join my people, that great number that have died,
    whom in their death Persephone received.
    I am the last of them and I go down
    in the worst death of all—for I have not lived   950
    the due term of my life. But when I come
    to that other world my hope is strong
    that my coming will be welcome to my father,
    and dear to you, my mother, and dear to you,
    my brother deeply loved. For when you died,
    with my own hands I washed and dressed you all,
    and poured the lustral offerings on your graves.

And now, Polyneices, it was for such care of your body
that I have earned these wages.
Yet those who think rightly will think I did right   960
in honoring you. Had I been a mother
of children, and my husband been dead and rotten,
I would not have taken this weary task upon me
against the will of the city. What law backs me
when I say this? I will tell you:
If my husband were dead, I might have had another,
and child from another man, if I lost the first.
But when father and mother both were hidden in death
no brother's life would bloom for me again.
That is the law under which I gave you precedence,   970
my dearest brother, and that is why Creon thinks me
wrong, even a criminal, and now takes me
by the hand and leads me away,
unbedded, without bridal, without share
in marriage and in nurturing of children;
as lonely as you see me; without friends;
with fate against me I go to the vault of death
while still alive. What law of God have I broken?
Why should I still look to the gods in my misery?
Whom should I summon as ally? For indeed   980
because of piety I was called impious.
If this proceeding is good in the gods' eyes
I shall know my sin, once I have suffered.
But if Creon and his people are the wrongdoers
let their suffering be no worse than the injustice
they are meting out to me.

Chorus

    It is the same blasts, the tempests of the soul,
    possess her.

Creon

                Then for this her guards,
    who are so slow, will find themselves in trouble.   990

Antigone *(cries out)*
    Oh, that word has come
    very close to death.

Creon
    I will not comfort you
    with hope that the sentence will not be accomplished.

Antigone
    O my father's city, in Theban land,
    O gods that sired my race,
    I am led away, I have no more stay.
    Look on me, princes of Thebes,
    the last remnant of the old royal line;
    see what I suffer and who makes me suffer   1000
    because I gave reverence to what claims reverence.

Chorus
    Danae suffered, too, when, her beauty lost, she gave
    the light of heaven in exchange for brassbound walls,
    and in the tomb-like cell was she hidden and held;
    yet she was honored in her breeding, child,
    and she kept, as guardian, the seed of Zeus
    that came to her in a golden shower.
    But there is some terrible power in destiny
    and neither wealth nor war
    nor tower nor black ships, beaten by the sea,   1010
    can give escape from it.

    The hot-tempered son of Dryas, the Edonian king,
    in fury mocked Dionysus,
    who then held him in restraint
    in a rocky dungeon.
    So the terrible force and flower of his madness
    drained away. He came to know the god
    whom in frenzy he had touched with his mocking tongue,
    when he would have checked the inspired women
    and the fire of Dionysus,   1020
    when he provoked the Muses that love the lyre.

By the black rocks, dividing the sea in two,
are the shores of the Bosporus, Thracian Salmydessus.
There the god of war who lives near the city
saw the terrible blinding wound
dealt by his savage wife
on Phineus' two sons.
She blinded and tore with the points of her shuttle,
and her bloodied hands, those eyes
that else would have looked on her vengefully.   1030
As they wasted away, they lamented
their unhappy fate that they were doomed
to be born of a mother cursed in her marriage.
She traced her descent from the seed
of the ancient Erechtheidae.
In far-distant caves she was raised
among her father's storms, that child of Boreas,
quick as a horse, over the steep hills,
a daughter of the gods.
But, my child, the long-lived Fates   1040
bore hard upon her, too.

(Enter Teiresias, the blind prophet, led by a boy.)

Teiresias
My lords of Thebes, we have come here together,
one pair of eyes serving us both. For the blind
such must be the way of going, by a guide's leading.

Creon
What is the news, my old Teiresias?

Teiresias
I will tell you; and you, listen to the prophet.

Creon
Never in the past have I turned from your advice.

Teiresias
And so you have steered well the ship of state.

Creon
    I have benefited and can testify to that.

Teiresias
    Then realize you are on the razor edge   1050
    of danger.

Creon
    What can that be? I shudder to hear those words.

Teiresias
    When you learn the signs recognized by my art
    you will understand.
    I sat at my ancient place of divination
    for watching the birds, where every bird finds shelter;
    and I heard an unwonted voice among them;
    they were horribly distressed, and screamed unmeaningly.
    I knew they were tearing each other murderously;
    the beating of their wings was a clear sign.   1060
    I was full of fear; at once on all the altars,
    as they were fully kindled, I tasted the offerings,
    but the god of fire refused to burn from the sacrifice,
    and from the thighbones a dark stream of moisture
    oozed from the embers, smoked and sputtered.
    The gall bladder burst and scattered to the air
    and the streaming thighbones lay exposed
    from the fat wrapped round them—
    so much I learned from this boy here,
    the fading prophecies of a rite that failed.   1070
    This boy here is my guide, as I am others'.
    This is the city's sickness—and your plans are the cause of it.
    For our altars and our sacrificial hearths
    are filled with the carrion meat of birds and dogs,
    torn from the flesh of Oedipus' poor son.
    So the gods will not take our prayers or sacrifice
    nor yet the flame from the thighbones, and no bird
    cries shrill and clear, so glutted
    are they with fat of the blood of the killed man.

Reflect on these things, son. All men
can make mistakes; but, once mistaken,
a man is no longer stupid nor accursed
who, having fallen on ill, tries to cure that ill,
not taking a fine undeviating stand.
It is obstinacy that convicts of folly.
Yield to the dead man; do not stab him—
now he is gone—what bravery is this,
to inflict another death upon the dead?
I mean you well and speak well for your good.
It is never sweeter to learn from a good counselor
than when he counsels to your benefit.

1090

Creon

Old man, you are all archers, and I am your mark.
I must be tried by your prophecies as well.
By the breed of you I have been bought and sold
and made a merchandise, for ages now.
But I tell you: make your profit from silver-gold
from Sardis and the gold from India
if you will. But this dead man you shall not hide
in a grave, not though the eagles of Zeus should bear
the carrion, snatching it to the throne of Zeus itself.
Even so, I shall not so tremble at the pollution
to let you bury him.

1100

No, I am certain
no human has the power to pollute the gods.
They fall, you old Teiresias, those men,
—so very clever—in a bad fall whenever
they eloquently speak vile words for profit.

Teiresias

I wonder if there's a man who dares consider—

Creon

What do you mean? What sort of generalization
is this talk of yours?

1110

Teiresias
How much the best of possessions is the ability
to listen to wise advice?

Creon
As I should imagine that the worst
injury must be native stupidity.

Teiresias
Now that is exactly where your mind is sick.

Creon
I do not like to answer a seer with insults.

Teiresias
But you do, when you say my prophecies are lies.

Creon
Well,
the whole breed of prophets certainly loves money.

Teiresias
And the breed that comes from princes loves to take
advantage—base advantage.   1120

Creon
                              Do you realize
you are speaking in such terms of your own prince?

Teiresias
I know. But it is through me you have saved the city.

Creon
You are a wise prophet, but what you love is wrong.

Teiresias
You will force me to declare what should be hidden
in my own heart.

Creon
                    Out with it—
but only if your words are not for gain.

Teiresias
  They won't be for *your* gain—that I am sure of.

Creon
  But realize you will not make a merchandise   1130
  of my decisions.

Teiresias
                        And you must realize
  that you will not outlive many cycles more
  of this swift sun before you give in exchange
  one of your own loins bred, a corpse for a corpse,
  for you have thrust one that belongs above
  below the earth, and bitterly dishonored
  a living soul by lodging her in the grave;
  while one that belonged indeed to the underworld
  gods you have kept on this earth without due share   1140
  of rites of burial, of due funeral offerings,
  a corpse unhallowed. With all of this you, Creon,
  have nothing to do, nor have the gods above.
  These acts of yours are violence, on your part.
  And in requital the avenging Spirits
  of Death itself and the gods' Furies shall
  after *your* deeds, lie in ambush for you, and
  in their hands you shall be taken cruelly.
  Now, look at this and tell me I was bribed
  to say it! The delay will not be long   1150
  before the cries of mourning in your house,
  of men and women. All the cities will stir in hatred
  against you, because their sons in mangled shreds
  received their burial rites from dogs, from wild beasts
  or when some bird of the air brought a vile stink
  to each city that contained the hearths of the dead.
  These are the arrows that archer-like I launched—
  you vexed me so to anger—at your heart.
  You shall not escape their sting. You, boy,

lead me away to my house, so he may discharge   1160
his anger on younger men; so may he come to know
to bear a quieter tongue in his head and a better
mind than that now he carries in him.

Chorus

That was a terrible prophecy, my lord.
The man has gone. Since these hairs of mine grew white
from the black they once were, he has never spoken
a word of a lie to our city.

Creon

I know, I know.
My mind is all bewildered. To yield is terrible.
But by opposition to destroy my very being
with a self-destructive curse must also be reckoned   1170
in what is terrible.

Chorus

You need good counsel, son of Menoeceus,
and need to take it.

Creon

What must I do, then? Tell me; I shall agree.

Chorus

The girl—go now and bring her up from her cave,
and for the exposed dead man, give him his burial.

Creon

That is really your advice? You would have me yield.

Chorus

And quickly as you may, my lord. Swift harms
sent by the gods cut off the paths of the foolish.

Creon

Oh, it is hard; I must give up what my heart   1180
would have me do. But it is ill to fight
against what must be.

Chorus

Go now, and do this;
do not give the task to others.

Creon

I will go,
just as I am. Come, servants, all of you;
take axes in your hands; away with you
to the place you see, there.
For my part, since my intention is so changed,
as I bound her myself, myself will free her.   1190
I am afraid it may be best, in the end
of life, to have kept the old accepted laws.

Chorus

You of many names, glory of the Cadmeian
bride, breed of loud thundering Zeus;
you who watch over famous Italy;
you who rule where all are welcome in Eleusis;
in the sheltered plains of Deo—
O Bacchus that dwells in Thebes,
the mother city of Bacchanals,
by the flowing stream of Ismenus,   1200
in the ground sown by the fierce dragon's teeth.

You are he on whom the murky gleam of torches glares,
above the twin peaks of the crag
where come the Corycean nymphs
to worship you, the Bacchanals;
and the stream of Castalia has seen you, too;
and you are he that the ivy-clad
slopes of Nisaean hills,
and the green shore ivy-clustered,
sent to watch over the roads of Thebes,   1210
where the immortal Evoe chant rings out.

It is Thebes which you honor most of all cities,
you and your mother both,
she who died by the blast of Zeus' thunderbolt.

And now when the city, with all its folk,
is gripped by a violent plague,
come with healing foot, over the slopes of Parnassus,
over the moaning strait.
You lead the dance of the fire-breathing stars,
you are master of the voices of the night.   1220
True-born child of Zeus, appear,
my lord, with your Thyiad attendants,
who in frenzy all night long
dance in your house, Iacchus,
dispenser of gifts.

Messenger
You who live by the house of Cadmus and Amphion,
hear me. There is no condition of man's life
that stands secure. As such I would not
praise it or blame. It is chance that sets upright;
it is chance that brings down the lucky and the unlucky,   1230
each in his turn. For men, that belong to death,
there is no prophet of established things.
Once Creon was a man worthy of envy—
of my envy, at least. For he saved this city
of Thebes from her enemies, and attained
the throne of the land, with all a king's power.
He guided it right. His race bloomed
with good children. But when a man forfeits joy
I do not count his life as life, but only
a life trapped in a corpse.   1240
Be rich within your house, yes greatly rich,
if so you will, and live in a prince's style.
If the gladness of these things is gone, I would not
give the shadow of smoke for the rest,
as against joy.

Chorus
What is the sorrow of our princes
of which you are the messenger?

Messenger

Death; and the living are guilty of their deaths.

Chorus

But who is the murderer? Who the murdered? Tell us.

Messenger

Haemon is dead; the hand that shed his blood   1250
was his very own.

Chorus

Truly his own hand? Or his father's?

Messenger

His own hand, in his anger
against his father for a murder.

Chorus

Prophet, how truly you have made good your word!

Messenger

These things are so; you may debate the rest.
Here I see Creon's wife Eurydice
approaching. Unhappy woman!
Does she come from the house as hearing about her son
or has she come by chance?   1260

Eurydice

I heard your words, all you men of Thebes, as I
was going out to greet Pallas with my prayers.
I was just drawing back the bolts of the gate
to open it when a cry struck through my ears
telling of my household's ruin. I fell backward
in terror into the arms of my servants; I fainted.
But tell me again, what is the story? I
will hear it as one who is no stranger to sorrow.

Messenger

Dear mistress, I will tell you, for I was there,
and I will leave out no word of the truth.   1270

Why should I comfort you and then tomorrow
be proved a liar? The truth is always best.

I followed your husband, at his heels, to the end of the plain
where Polyneices' body still lay unpitied,
and torn by dogs. We prayed to Hecate, goddess
of the crossroads, and also to Pluto
that they might restrain their anger and turn kind.
And him we washed with sacred lustral water
and with fresh-cut boughs we burned what was left of him
and raised a high mound of his native earth;   1280
then we set out again for the hollowed rock,
death's stone bridal chamber for the girl.
Someone then heard a voice of bitter weeping
while we were still far off, coming from that unblest room.
The man came to tell our master Creon of it.
As the king drew nearer, there swarmed about him
a cry of misery but no clear words.
He groaned and in an anguished mourning voice
cried "Oh, am I a true prophet? Is this the road
that I must travel, saddest of all my wayfaring?   1290
It is my son's voice that haunts my ear. Servants,
get closer, quickly. Stand around the tomb
and look. There is a gap there where the stones
have been wrenched away; enter there, by the very mouth,
and see whether I recognize the voice of Haemon
or if the gods deceive me." On the command
of our despairing master we went to look.
In the furthest part of the tomb we saw her, hanging
by her neck. She had tied a noose of muslin on it.
Haemon's hands were about her waist embracing her,   1300
while he cried for the loss of his bride gone to the dead,
and for all his father had done, and his own sad love.
When Creon saw him he gave a bitter cry,
went in and called to him with a groan: "Poor son!
what have you done? What can you have meant?

What happened to destroy you? Come out, I pray you!"
The boy glared at him with savage eyes, and then
spat in his face, without a word of answer.
He drew his double-hilted sword. As his father
ran to escape him, Haemon failed to strike him,   1310
and the poor wretch in anger at himself
leaned on his sword and drove it halfway in,
into his ribs. Then he folded the girl to him,
in his arms, while he was conscious still,
and gasping poured a sharp stream of bloody drops
on her white cheeks. There they lie,
the dead upon the dead. So he has won
the pitiful fulfillment of his marriage
within death's house. In this human world he has shown
how the wrong choice in plans is for a man   1320
his greatest evil.

Chorus
  What do you make of this? My lady is gone,
  without a word of good or bad.

Messenger
                    I, too,
  am lost in wonder. I am inclined to hope
  that hearing of her son's death she could not
  open her sorrow to the city, but chose rather
  within her house to lay upon her maids
  the mourning for the household grief. Her judgment
  is good; she will not make any false step.   1330

Chorus
  I do not know. To me this over-heavy silence
  seems just as dangerous as much empty wailing.

Messenger
  I will go in and learn if in her passionate
  heart she keeps hidden some secret purpose.
  You are right; there is sometimes danger in too much silence.

Chorus

    Here comes our king himself. He bears in his hands
    a memorial all too clear;
    it is a ruin of none other's making,
    purely his own if one dare to say that.

Creon

    The mistakes of a blinded man   1340
    are themselves rigid and laden with death.
    You look at us the killer and the killed
    of the one blood. Oh, the awful blindness
    of those plans of mine. My son, you were so young,
    so young to die. You were freed from the bonds of life
    through no folly of your own—only through mine.

Chorus

    I think you have learned justice—but too late.

Creon

    Yes, I have learned it to my bitterness. At this moment
    God has sprung on my head with a vast weight
    and struck me down. He shook me in my savage ways;   1350
    he has overturned my joy, has trampled it,
    underfoot. The pains men suffer
    are pains indeed.

Second Messenger

    My lord, you have troubles and a store besides;
    some are there in your hands, but there are others
    you will surely see when you come to your house.

Creon

    What trouble can there be beside these troubles?

Second Messenger

    The queen is dead. She was indeed true mother
    of the dead son. She died, poor lady,
    by recent violence upon herself.   1360

Creon

    Haven of death, you can never have enough.
    Why, why do you destroy me?
    You messenger, who have brought me bitter news,
    what is this tale you tell?
    It is a dead man that you kill again—
    what new message of yours is this, boy?
    Is this new slaughter of a woman
    a doom to lie on the pile of the dead?

Chorus

    You can see. It is no longer
    hidden in a corner.   1370

    (By some stage device, perhaps the so-called eccyclema, the inside of
             the palace is shown, with the body of the dead Queen.)

Creon

    Here is yet another horror
    for my unhappy eyes to see.
    What doom still waits for me?
    I have but now taken in my arms my son,
    and again I look upon another dead face.
    Poor mother and poor son!

Second Messenger

    She stood at the altar, and with keen whetted knife
    she suffered her darkening eyes to close.
    First she cried in agony recalling the noble fate of Megareus,
    who died before all this,   1380
    and then for the fate of this son; and in the end
    she cursed you for the evil you had done
    in killing her sons.

Creon

    I am distracted with fear. Why does not someone
    strike a two-edged sword right through me?
    I am dissolved in an agony of misery.

Second Messenger
    You were indeed accused
    by her that is dead
    of Haemon's and of Megareus' death.

Creon
    By what kind of violence did she find her end?   1390

Second Messenger
    Her own hand struck her to the entrails
    when she heard of her son's lamentable death.

Creon
    These acts can never be made to fit another
    to free me from the guilt. It was I that killed her.
    Poor wretch that I am, I say it is true!
    Servants, lead me away, quickly, quickly.
    I am no more a live man than one dead.

Chorus
    What you say is for the best—if there be a best
    in evil such as this. For the shortest way
    is best with troubles that lie at our feet.   1400

Creon
    O, let it come, let it come,
    that best of fates that waits on my last day.
    Surely best fate of all. Let it come, let it come!
    That I may never see one more day's light!

Chorus
    These things are for the future. We must deal
    with what impends. What in the future is to care for
    rests with those whose duty it is
    to care for them.

Creon
    At least, all that *I* want
    is in that prayer of mine.   1410

Chorus

    Pray for no more at all. For what is destined
    for us, men mortal, there is no escape.

Creon

    Lead me away, a vain silly man
    who killed you, son, and you, too, lady.
    I did not mean to, but I did.
    I do not know where to turn my eyes
    to look to, for support.
    Everything in my hands is crossed. A most unwelcome fate
    has leaped upon me.

Chorus

    Wisdom is far the chief element in happiness   1420
    and, secondly, no irreverence towards the gods.
    But great words of haughty men exact
    in retribution blows as great
    and in old age teach wisdom.

HIPPOLYTUS

Translated by David Grene

INTRODUCTION

Hippolytus was presented in 428 B.C. and won first prize. It is, however, a second version; a previous *Hippolytus* (lost) had been con-
sidered "scandalous" and was badly received. Sophocles used the
same story in his *Phaedra*. This is lost, and there is no clue to its date.
Seneca in his *Phaedra*, Racine in his *Phèdre*, O'Neill in his *Desire under
the Elms*, and Jeffers in his *Cawdor* have, in their own ways, retold
the story.

Theseus, king of Athens, had an illegitimate son by an Amazon,
Hippolytus. Late in life he married a young wife, Phaedra, princess
of Crete, who bore him two sons. Phaedra fell in love with Hippolytus, and her desire was communicated to him. He rejected it, and
Phaedra (in this version, by means of a suicide note) told Theseus
that Hippolytus had attacked her. Theseus caused his son's death by
praying to his own father, Poseidon, to destroy him. But Artemis
revealed the truth and established the cult of Hippolytus as a divinity
of nature.

This story of the young man tempted and traduced has many
parallels in Greek legend, and also in the biblical story of Joseph and
the wife of Potiphar. The parallels, however, involve the prompt
vindication of the hero and launch him on a career of heroic ex-
ploits. The woman in the case figures only as a temptress. Euripides
has gone with great sympathy into the feelings of Phaedra, a helpless victim of her passions (Aphrodite) whose mind clings despite
all to its integrity. Hippolytus too has his ideals. His seraphic love
for the unattainable goddess Artemis displays at the same time his
admiration for beauty and his dislike of sex. But the quarrel between
sacred and profane love, represented by Artemis and Aphrodite,
thwarts the good purposes of the human persons and wrecks both
lives.

CHARACTERS

Theseus

Hippolytus, his son by the queen of the Amazons

Phaedra, Theseus' wife, stepmother to Hippolytus

A Servant

A Messenger

The Nurse

The Chorus of Palace women, natives of Troezen

A Chorus of huntsmen, in attendance on Hippolytus

The Goddess Aphrodite

The Goddess Artemis

HIPPOLYTUS

SCENE: *Troezen, in front of the house of Theseus.*

PROLOGUE

Aphrodite

I am called the Goddess Cypris:
I am mighty among men and they honor me by many names.
All those that live and see the light of sun
from Atlas' Pillars to the tide of Pontus
are mine to rule.   5
Such as worship my power in all humility,
I exalt in honor.
But those whose pride is stiff-necked against me
I lay by the heels.
There is joy in the heart of a God also
when honored by men.

Now I will quickly tell you the truth of this story.

Hippolytus, son of Theseus by the Amazon,   10
pupil of holy Pittheus,
alone among the folk of this land of Troezen has blasphemed me
counting me vilest of the Gods in Heaven.
He will none of the bed of love nor marriage,
but honors Artemis, Zeus's daughter,   15
counting her greatest of the Gods in Heaven
he is with her continually, this Maiden Goddess, in the greenwood.
They hunt with hounds and clear the land of wild things,
mortal with immortal in companionship.
I do not grudge him such privileges: why should I?   20
But for his sins against me
I shall punish Hippolytus this day.
I have no need to toil to win my end:
much of the task has been already done.

Once he came from Pittheus' house[1] to the country of Pandion
that he might see and be initiate in the holy mysteries.   25
Phaedra saw him
and her heart was filled with the longings of love.
This was my work.
So before ever she came to Troezen
close to the rock of Pallas in view of this land,   30
she dedicated a temple to Cypris.
For her love, too, dwelt in a foreign land.
Ages to come will call this temple after him,
the temple of the Goddess established here.
When Theseus left the land of Cecrops,
flying from the guilty stain of the murder of the Pallantids,   35
condemning himself to a year's exile
he sailed with his wife to this land.
Phaedra groans in bitterness of heart
and the goads of love prick her cruelly,
and she is like to die.
But she breathes not a word of her secret and none of the servants   40
know of the sickness that afflicts her.
But her love shall not remain thus aimless and unknown.
I will reveal the matter to Theseus and all shall come out.
Father shall slay son with curses—
this son that is hateful to me.
For once the Lord Poseidon, Ruler of the Sea,
granted this favor to Theseus   45
that three of his prayers to the God should find answer.

1. "Pittheus' house": The historian Pausanias, relating the legend of Hippolytus,
says: "King Theseus, when he married Phaedra, daughter of the king of Crete, was in
a quandary what to do with Hippolytus, his son by his former mistress, Antiope the
Amazon. He did not wish that after his own death Hippolytus should rule the children
of his legitimate marriage, nor yet that Hippolytus should be ruled by them, for he
loved him. So he sent the boy to be brought up by his grandfather Pittheus, who lived
in Troezen and ruled there. Theseus hoped that when Pittheus died, Hippolytus might
inherit the kingdom, and thus peace within the family be preserved, Hippolytus gov-
erning Troezen, and Phaedra's children holding sway in Athens." "Pandion's country"
and "land of Cecrops" both signify Attica. Pandion and Cecrops were early legendary
heroes of Attica.

Renowned shall Phaedra be in her death, but none the less
die she must.
Her suffering does not weigh in the scale so much
that I should let my enemies go untouched
escaping payment of that retribution
that honor demands that I have.   50
Look, here is the son of Theseus, Hippolytus!
He has just left his hunting.
I must go away.
See the great crowd that throngs upon his heels
and shouts the praise of Artemis in hymns!   55
He does not know
that the doors of death are open for him,
that he is looking on his last sun.

SCENE I

*(Enter Hippolytus, attended by friends and servants carrying
nets, hunting spears, etc.)*

Hippolytus

Follow me singing
the praises of Artemis,
Heavenly One, Child of Zeus,
Artemis!
We are the wards of your care.   60

(The Chorus of huntsmen chant.)

Hail, Holy and Gracious!
Hail, Daughter of Zeus!
Hail, Maiden Daughter of Zeus and Leto!   65
Dweller in the spacious sky!
Maid of the Mighty Father!
Maid of the Golden Glistening House!
Hail!
Maiden Goddess most beautiful of all the Heavenly Host that
lives in Olympus!   70

*(Hippolytus advances to the altar of Artemis and
lays a garland on it, praying.)*

My Goddess Mistress, I bring you ready woven
this garland. It was I that plucked and wove it,
plucked it for you in your inviolate Meadow.
No shepherd dares to feed his flock within it: 75
no reaper plies a busy scythe within it:
only the bees in springtime haunt the inviolate Meadow.
Its gardener is the spirit Reverence who
refreshes it with water from the river.
Not those who by instruction have profited
to learn, but in whose very soul the seed   80
of Chastity toward all things alike
nature has deeply rooted, they alone
may gather flowers there! the wicked may not.

Loved mistress, here I offer you this coronal;
it is a true worshipper's hand that gives it you
to crown the golden glory of your hair.
With no man else I share this privilege
that I am with you and to your words   85
can answer words. True, I may only hear:
I may not see God face to face.
So may I turn the post set at life's end
even as I began the race.

Servant
    King—for I will not call you "Master," that belongs
    to the Gods only—will you take good advice?

Hippolytus
    Certainly I will take good advice. I am not a fool.   90

Servant
    In men's communities one rule holds good,
    do you know it, King?

Hippolytus
                    Not I. What is this rule?
Servant
    Men hate the haughty of heart who will not be
    the friend of every man.

Hippolytus

> And rig~~h~~ ~~t~~oo:
For haughty heart breeds arrogant demeanor.

Servant

And affability wins favor, then?

Hippolytus

Abundant favor. Aye, and profit, too,
at little cost of trouble.

Servant

> Do you think
that it's the same among the Gods in Heaven?

Hippolytus

If we in our world and the Gods in theirs
know the same usages—Yes.

Servant

> Then, King, how comes it
that for a holy Goddess you have not even
a word of salutation?

Hippolytus

> Which Goddess?
Be careful, or you will find that tongue of yours
may make a serious mistake.

Servant

> This Goddess here
who stands before your gates, the Goddess Cypris.

Hippolytus

I worship her—but from a long way off,
for I am chaste.

Servant

> Yet she's a holy Goddess,
and fair is her renown throughout the world.

Hippolytus

Men make their choice: one man honors one God,
and one another.

Servant
> Well, good fortune guard you!
> if you have the mind you should have.   105

Hippolytus
> God of nocturnal prowess is not my God.

Servant
> The honors of the Gods you must not scant, my son.

Hippolytus
> Go, men, into the house and look to supper.
> A plentiful table is an excellent thing
> after the hunt. And you (*singing out two*) rub down my horses.   110
> When I have eaten I shall exercise them.
> For your Cypris here—a long goodbye to her!

> > (*The old man is left standing alone on the stage.*
> > *He prays before the statue of Aphrodite.*)

> O Cypris Mistress, we must not imitate
> the young men when they have such thoughts as these.
> As fits a slave to speak, here at your image   115
> I bow and worship. You should grant forgiveness
> when one that has a young tempestuous heart
> speaks foolish words. Seem not to hear them.
> You should be wiser than mortals, being Gods.   120

> > (*Enter Chorus of women, servants in Phaedra's house.*)

Chorus

STROPHE

> There is a rock streaming with water,
> whose source, men say, is Ocean,
> and it pours from the heart of its stone a spring
> where pitchers may dip and be filled.
> My friend was there and in the river water   125
> she dipped and washed the royal purple robes,
> and spread them on the rock's warm back
> where the sunbeams played.

It was from her I heard at first
of the news of my mistress' sorrow.   130

ANTISTROPHE

She lies on her bed within the house,
within the house and fever wracks her
and she hides her golden head in fine-spun robes.
This is the third day   135
she has eaten no bread
and her body is pure and fasting.
For she would willingly bring her life to anchor
at the end of its voyage
the gloomy harbor of death.   140

STROPHE

Is it Pan's frenzy that possesses you
or is Hecate's madness upon you, maid?
Can it be the holy Corybantes,
or the mighty Mother who rules the mountains?
Are you wasted in suffering thus,   145
for a sin against Dictynna, Queen of hunters?
Are you perhaps unhallowed, having offered
no sacrifice to her from taken victims?
For she goes through the waters of the Lake[2]
can travel on dry land beyond the sea,
the eddying salt sea.   150

ANTISTROPHE

Can it be that some other woman's love,
a secret love that hides itself from you,
has beguiled your husband
the son of Erechtheus
our sovran lord, that prince of noble birth?
Or has some sailor from the shores of Crete   155

2. Limnae, the Lake, a district in Laconia, was the center of the worship of Artemis
in the Peloponnese. From it she is sometimes called Limnaios, or Lady of the Lake.

put in at this harbor hospitable to sailors,
bearing a message for our queen,
and so because he told her some calamity
her spirit is bound in chains of grief
and she lies on her bed in sorrow?   160

EPODE

Unhappy is the compound of woman's nature;
the torturing misery of helplessness,
the helplessness of childbirth and its madness
are linked to it for ever.
My body, too, has felt this thrill of pain,   165
and I called on Artemis, Queen of the Bow;
she has my reverence always
as she goes in the company of the Gods.

But here is the old woman, the queen's nurse   170
here at the door. She is bringing her mistress out.
There is a gathering cloud upon her face.
What is the matter? my soul is eager to know.
What can have made the queen so pale?
What can have wasted her body so?   175

SCENE II

(Enter the Nurse, supporting Phaedra.)

Nurse

A weary thing is sickness and its pains!
What must I do now?
Here is light and air, the brightness of the sky.
I have brought out the couch on which you tossed
in fever—here clear of the house.   180
Your every word has been to bring you out,
but when you're here, you hurry in again.
You find no constant pleasure anywhere
for when your joy is upon you, suddenly
you're foiled and cheated.
There's no content for you in what you have
for you're forever finding something dearer,

some other thing—because you have it not.   185
It's better to be sick than nurse the sick.
Sickness is single trouble for the sufferer:
but nursing means vexation of the mind,
and hard work for the hands besides.
The life of man entire is misery:
he finds no resting place, no haven from calamity.   190
But something other dearer still than life
the darkness hides and mist encompasses;
we are proved luckless lovers of this thing
that glitters in the underworld: no man
can tell us of the stuff of it, expounding   195
what is, and what is not: we know nothing of it.
Idly we drift, on idle stories carried.

Phaedra (to the servants)

Lift me up! Lift my head up! All the muscles
are slack and useless. Here, you, take my hands.
They're beautiful, my hands and arms!   200
Take away this hat! It is too heavy to wear.
Take it away! Let my hair fall free on my shoulders.

Nurse

Quiet, child, quiet! Do not so restlessly
keep tossing to and fro! It's easier
to bear an illness if you have some patience   205
and the spirit of good breeding.
We all must suffer sometimes: we are mortal.

Phaedra

O,
if I could only draw from the dewy spring
a draught of fresh spring water!
If I could only lie beneath the poplars,   210
in the tufted meadow and find my rest there!

Nurse

Child, why do you rave so? There are others here.

Cease tossing out these wild demented words
whose driver is madness.

Phaedra

Bring me to the mountains! I *will* go to the mountains! 215
Among the pine trees where the huntsmen's pack
trails spotted stags and hangs upon their heels.
God, how I long to set the hounds on, shouting!
And poise the Thessalian javelin drawing it back—
here where my fair hair hangs above the ear— 220
I would hold in my hand a spear with a steel point.

Nurse

What ails you, child? What is this love of hunting,
and you a lady! Draught of fresh spring water!
Here, beside the tower there is a sloping ridge 225
with springs enough to satisfy your thirst.

Phaedra

Artemis, mistress of the Salty Lake,
mistress of the ring echoing to the racers' hoofs,
if only I could gallop your level stretches, 230
and break Venetian colts!

Nurse

This is sheer madness,
that prompts such whirling, frenzied, senseless words.
Here at one moment you're afire with longing
to hunt wild beasts and you'd go to the hills,
and then again all your desire is horses,
horses on the sands beyond the reach of the breakers. 235
Indeed, it would need to be a mighty prophet
to tell which of the Gods mischievously
jerks you from your true course and thwarts your wits!

Phaedra

O, I am miserable! What is this I've done?
Where have I strayed from the highway of good sense? 240
I was mad. It was the madness sent from some God

that caused my fall.
I am unhappy, so unhappy! Nurse,
cover my face again. I am ashamed   245
of what I said. Cover me up. The tears
are flowing, and my face is turned to shame.
Rightness of judgment is bitterness to the heart.
Madness is terrible. It is better then
that I should die and know no more of anything.

Nurse

There, now, you are covered up. But my own body   250
when will death cover that? I have learned much
from my long life. The mixing bowl of friendship,
the love of one for the other, must be tempered.
Love must not touch the marrow of the soul.   255
Our affections must be breakable chains that we
can cast them off or tighten them.
That one soul so for two should be in travail
as I for her, that is a heavy burden.   260
The ways of life that are most fanatical
trip us up more, they say, than bring us joy.
They're enemies to health. So I praise less
the extreme than temperance in everything.   265
The wise will bear me out.

Chorus Leader

Old woman, you are Phaedra's faithful nurse.
We can see that she is in trouble but the cause
that ails her is black mystery to us.
We would like to hear you tell us what is the matter.   270

Nurse

I have asked and know no more. She will not tell me.

Chorus Leader

Not even what began it?

Nurse

                              And my answer
is still the same: of all this she will not speak.

Chorus Leader

But see how ill she is, and how her body
is wracked and wasted!

Nurse

                              Yes, she has eaten nothing
for two days now.   275

Chorus Leader

                    Is this the scourge of madness?
Or can it be . . . that death is what she seeks?

Nurse

Aye, death. She is starving herself to death.

Chorus Leader

I wonder that her husband suffers this.

Nurse

She hides her troubles, swears that she isn't sick.

Chorus Leader

But does he not look into her face and see   280
a witness that disproves her?

Nurse

                              No, he is gone.
He is away from home, in foreign lands.

Chorus Leader

Why, you must force her then to find the cause
of this mind-wandering sickness!

Nurse

                              Every means
I have tried and still have won no foot of ground.
But I'll not give up trying, even now.   285
You are here and can in person bear me witness
that I am loyal to my masters always,
even in misfortune's hour.
Dear child, let us both forget our former words.
Be kinder, you: unknit that ugly frown.

For my part I will leave this track of thought:　　　290
I cannot understand you there. I'll take
another and a better argument.

If you are sick and it is some secret sickness,
here are women standing at your side to help.
But if your troubles may be told to men,　　　295
speak, that a doctor may pronounce upon it.
So, not a word! Oh, why will you not speak?
There is no remedy in silence, child.
Either I am wrong and then you should correct me:
or right, and you should yield to what I say.
Say something! Look at me!　　　300

Women, I have tried and tried and all for nothing.
We are as far as ever from our goal.
It was the same before. She was not melted
by anything I said. She would not obey me.

But this you shall know, though to my reasoning
you are more dumbly obstinate than the sea:
If you die, you will be a traitor to your children.　　　305
They will never know their share in a father's palace.
No, by the Amazon Queen, the mighty rider
who bore a master for your children, one
bastard in birth but true-born son in mind,
you know him well—Hippolytus. . . .
　　　　　　　　　So that has touched you?　　　310

Phaedra

　You have killed me, nurse. For God's sake, I entreat you,
　never again speak that man's name to me.

Nurse

　You see? You have come to your senses, yet despite that,
　you will not make your children happy nor
　save your own life besides.

Phaedra
                  I love my children.
It is another storm of fate that batters me.   315

Nurse
There is no stain of blood upon your hands?

Phaedra
My hands are clean: the stain is in my heart.

Nurse
The hurt comes from outside? Some enemy?

Phaedra
One I love destroys me. Neither of us wills it.

Nurse
Has Theseus sinned a sin against you then?   320

Phaedra
God keep me equally guiltless in his sight!

Nurse
What is this terror urging you to death?

Phaedra
Leave me to my sins. My sins are not against you.

Nurse
Not of my will, but yours, you cast me off.

Phaedra
Would you force confession, my hand-clasping suppliant?   325

Nurse
Your knees too—and my hands will never free you.

Phaedra
Sorrow, nurse, sorrow, you will find my secret.

Nurse
Can I know greater sorrow than losing you?

Phaedra

You will kill me. My honor lies in silence.

Nurse

And then you will hide this honor, though I beseech you?   330

Phaedra

Yes, for I seek to win good out of shame.

Nurse

Where honor is, speech will make you more honorable.

Phaedra

O God, let go my hand and go away!

Nurse

No, for you have not given me what you should.

Phaedra

I yield. Your suppliant hand compels my reverence.   335

Nurse

I will say no more. Yours is the word from now.

Phaedra

Unhappy mother, what a love was yours!

Nurse

It is her love for the bull you mean, dear child?

Phaedra

Unhappy sister, bride of Dionysus!

Nurse

Why these ill-boding words about your kin?   340

Phaedra

And I the unlucky third, see how I end!

Nurse

Your words are wounds. Where will your tale conclude?

Phaedra

Mine is an inherited curse. It is not new.

Nurse

I have not yet heard what I most want to know.

Phaedra

If you could say for me what I must say for myself. 345

Nurse

I am no prophet to know your hidden secrets.

Phaedra

What is this thing, this love, of which they speak?

Nurse

Sweetest and bitterest, both in one, at once.

Phaedra

One of the two, the bitterness, I've known.

Nurse

Are you in love, my child? And who is he? 350

Phaedra

There is a man, . . . his mother was an Amazon. . . .

Nurse

You mean Hippolytus?

Phaedra

                You
have spoken it, not I.

Nurse

What do you mean? This is my death.
Women, this is past bearing. I'll not bear
life after this. A curse upon the daylight!
A curse upon this shining sun above us! 355
I'll throw myself from a cliff, throw myself headlong!
I'll be rid of life somehow, I'll die somehow!
Farewell to all of you! This is the end for me.

The chaste, they love not vice of their own will,
but yet they love it. Cypris, you are no God.

You are something stronger than God if that can be.   360
You have ruined her and me and all this house.

(*The Nurse goes off. The Chorus forms into two half-choruses.*)

First Half-chorus

Did you hear, did you hear
the queen crying aloud,
telling of a calamity
which no ear should hear?

Second Half-chorus

I would rather die
than think such thoughts as hers.   365

First Half-chorus

I am sorry for her trouble.

Second Half-chorus

Alas for troubles, man-besetting.

First Half-chorus (*turning to Phaedra*)

You are dead, you yourself
have dragged your ruin to the light.
What can happen now in the long
dragging stretch of the rest of your days?
Some new thing will befall the house.   370

Chorus (*united*)

We know now, we know now
how your love will end,
poor unhappy Cretan girl!

Phaedra

Hear me, you women of Troezen who live
in this extremity of land, this anteroom to Argos.
Many a time in night's long empty spaces   375
I have pondered on the causes of a life's shipwreck.
I think that our lives are worse than the mind's quality
would warrant. There are many who know virtue.

We know the good, we apprehend it clearly.   380
But we can't bring it to achievement. Some
are betrayed by their own laziness, and others
value some other pleasure above virtue.
There are many pleasures in a woman's life—
long gossiping talks and leisure, that sweet curse.
Then there is shame that thwarts us. Shame is of two kinds.   385
The one is harmless, but the other a plague.
For clarity's sake, we should not talk of "shame,"
a single word for two quite different things.
These then are my thoughts. Nothing can now seduce me   390
to the opposite opinion. I will tell you
in my own case the track which my mind followed.
At first when love had struck me, I reflected
how best to bear it. Silence was my first plan.
Silence and concealment. For the tongue
is not to be trusted: it can criticize   395
another's faults, but on its own possessor
it brings a thousand troubles.
Then I believed that I could conquer love,
conquer it with discretion and good sense.
And when that too failed me, I resolved to die.   400
And death is the best plan of them all. Let none of you
dispute that.
It would always be my choice
to have my virtues known and honored. So
when I do wrong I could not endure to see
a circle of condemning witnesses.
I know what I have done: I know the scandal: 405
and all too well I know that I am a woman,
object of hate to all. Destruction light
upon the wife who herself plays the tempter
and strains her loyalty to her husband's bed
by dalliance with strangers. In the wives   410
of noble houses first this taint begins:
when wickedness approves itself to those

of noble birth, it will surely be approved
by their inferiors. Truly, too, I hate
lip-worshippers of chastity who own
a lecherous daring when they have privacy.
O Cypris, Sea-Born Goddess, how can they   415
look frankly in the faces of their husbands
and never shiver with fear lest their accomplice,
the darkness, and the rafters of the house
take voice and cry aloud?
This then, my friends, is my destruction:
I cannot bear that I should be discovered   420
a traitor to my husband and my children.
God grant them rich and glorious life in Athens—
famous Athens—freedom in word and deed,
and from their mother an honorable name.
It makes the stoutest-hearted man a slave
if in his soul he knows his parents' shame.   425

The proverb runs: "There is one thing alone
that stands the brunt of life throughout its course,
a quiet conscience," . . . a just and quiet conscience
whoever can attain it.
Time holds a mirror, as for a young girl,
and sometimes as occasion falls, he shows us
the ugly rogues of the world. I would not wish
that I should be seen among them.   430

Chorus Leader

How virtue is held lovely everywhere,
and harvests a good name among mankind!

(*The Nurse returns.*)

Nurse

Mistress, the trouble you have lately told me,
coming on me so suddenly, frightened me;
but now I realize that I was foolish.   435
In this world second thoughts, it seems, are best.
Your case is not so extraordinary,

beyond thought or reason. The Goddess in her anger
has smitten you, and you are in love. What wonder
is this? There are many thousands suffer with you.
So, you will die for love! And all the others,   440
who love, and who will love, must they die, too?
How will that profit them? The tide of love,
at its full surge, is not withstandable.
Upon the yielding spirit she comes gently,
but to the proud and the fanatic heart   445
she is a torturer with the brand of shame.
She wings her way through the air; she is in the sea,
in its foaming billows; from her everything,
that is, is born. For she engenders us
and sows the seed of desire whereof we're born,   450
all we her children, living on the earth.
He who has read the writings of the ancients
and has lived much in books, he knows
that Zeus once loved the lovely Semele;
he knows that Dawn, the bright light of the world,
once ravished Cephalus hence to the God's company   455
for love's sake. Yet all these dwell in heaven.
They are content, I am sure, to be subdued
by the stroke of love.
But you, you won't submit! Why, you should certainly
have had your father beget you on fixed terms   460
or with other Gods for masters, if you don't like
the laws that rule this world. Tell me, how many
of the wise ones of the earth do you suppose
see with averted eyes their wives turned faithless;
how many erring sons have fathers helped
with secret loves? It is the wise man's part   465
to leave in darkness everything that is ugly.

We should not in the conduct of our lives
be too exacting. Look, see this roof here—
these overarching beams that span your house—

could builders with all their skill lay them dead straight?
You've fallen into the great sea of love
and with your puny swimming would escape!   470
If in the sum you have more good luck than ill,
count yourself fortunate—for you are mortal.

Come, dear, give up your discontented mood.
Give up your railing. It's only insolent pride
to wish to be superior to the Gods.   475
Endure your love. The Gods have willed it so.
You are sick. Then try to find some subtle means
to turn your sickness into health again.
There are magic love charms, spells of enchantment;
we'll find some remedy for your love-sickness.
Men would take long to hunt devices out,   480
if we the women did not find them first.

Chorus Leader

Phaedra, indeed she speaks more usefully
for today's troubles. But it is you I praise.
And yet my praise brings with it more discomfort
than her words: it is bitterer to the ear.   485

Phaedra

This is the deadly thing which devastates
well-ordered cities and the homes of men—
that's it, this art of oversubtle words.
It's not the words ringing delight in the ear
that one should speak, but those that have the power
to save their hearer's honorable name.

Nurse

This is high moralizing! What you want   490
is not fine words, but the man! Come, let's be done.
And tell your story frankly and directly.
For if there were no danger to your life,
as now there is—or if you could be prudent,
I never would have led you on so far,   495

merely to please your fancy or your lust.
But now a great prize hangs on our endeavors,
and that's the saving of a life—yours, Phaedra,
there's none can blame us for our actions now.

Phaedra

What you say is wicked, wicked! Hold your tongue!
I will not hear such shameful words again.

Nurse

O, they are shameful! But they are better than   500
your noble-sounding moral sentiments.
"The deed" is better if it saves your life:
than your "good name" in which you die exulting.

Phaedra

For God's sake, do not press me any further!
What you say is true, but terrible!
My very soul is subdued by my love
and if you plead the cause of wrong so well   505
I shall fall into the abyss
from which I now am flying.

Nurse

If that is what you think, you should be virtuous.
But if you are not, obey me: that is next best.
It has just come to my mind, I have at home   510
some magic love charms. They will end your trouble;
they'll neither harm your honor nor your mind.
They'll end your trouble, . . . only you must be brave.   515

Phaedra

Is this a poison ointment or a drink?

Nurse

I don't know. Don't be overanxious, child,
to find out what it is. Accept its benefits.

Phaedra

I am afraid of you: I am afraid
that you will be too clever for my good.

Nurse

You are afraid of everything. What is it?

Phaedra

You surely will not tell this to Hippolytus?   520

Nurse

Come, let that be: I will arrange all well.
Only, my lady Cypris of the Sea,
be my helper you. The other plans I have
I'll tell to those we love within the house;
that will suffice.

(*The Nurse goes off.*)

Chorus

STROPHE

Love distills desire upon the eyes,   525
love brings bewitching grace into the heart
of those he would destroy.
I pray that love may never come to me
with murderous intent,
in rhythms measureless and wild.
Not fire nor stars have stronger bolts   530
than those of Aphrodite sent
by the hand of Eros, Zeus's child.

ANTISTROPHE

In vain by Alpheus' stream,   535
in vain in the halls of Phoebus' Pythian shrine
the land of Greece increases sacrifice.
But Love the King of Men they honor not,   540
although he keeps the keys
of the temple of desire,
although he goes destroying through the world,
author of dread calamities
and ruin when he enters human hearts.

STROPHE

The Oechalian maiden who had never known   545
the bed of love, known neither man nor marriage,

the Goddess Cypris gave to Heracles.
She took her from the home of Eurytus,
maiden unhappy in her marriage song,
wild as a Naiad or a Bacchanal,   550
with blood and fire, a murderous hymenaeal!

ANTISTROPHE

O holy walls of Thebes and Dirce's fountain   555
bear witness you, to Love's grim journeying:
once you saw Love bring Semele to bed,
lull her to sleep, clasped in the arms of Death,
pregnant with Dionysus by the thunder king.   560
Love is like a flitting bee in the world's garden
and for its flowers, destruction is in his breath.

SCENE III

(Phaedra is standing listening near the central door of the palace.)

Phaedra

Women, be silent!
                          (She listens and then recoils.)
Oh, I am destroyed forever.   565

Chorus Leader

What is there terrible within the house?

Phaedra

Hush, let me hear the voices within!

Chorus Leader

And I obey. But this is sorrow's prelude.

Phaedra (cries out)

Oh, I am the most miserable of women!   570

*(The Chorus Leader and the Chorus babble
excitedly among themselves.)*

What does she mean by her cries?
Why does she scream?
Tell us the fear-winged word, Mistress, the fear-winged word,
rushing upon the heart.

Phaedra

I am lost. Go, women, stand and listen there yourselves   575
and hear the tumult that falls on the house.

Chorus Leader

Mistress, you stand at the door.
It is you who can tell us best
what happens within the house.   580

Phaedra

Only the son of the horse-loving Amazon,
Hippolytus, cursing a servant maid.

Chorus Leader

My ears can catch a sound,   585
but I can hear nothing clear.
I can only hear a voice
scolding in anger.

Phaedra

It is plain enough. He cries aloud against
the mischievous bawd who betrays her mistress' love.   590

Chorus Leader

Lady, you are betrayed!
How can I help you?
What is hidden is revealed.
You are destroyed.
Those you love have betrayed you.   595

Phaedra

She loved me and she told him of my troubles,
and so has ruined me. She was my doctor,
but her cure has made my illness mortal now.

Chorus Leader

What will you do? There is no cure.

Phaedra

I know of one, and only one—quick death.
That is the only cure for my disease.   600

(*She retires into the palace through one of the side doors just as Hippolytus issues through the central door, dogged by the Nurse. Phaedra is conceived of as listening from behind her door during the entire conversation between the Nurse and Hippolytus.*)

Hippolytus

O Mother Earth! O Sun and open sky!
What words I have heard from this accursed tongue!

Nurse

Hush, son! Someone may hear you.

Hippolytus

You cannot
expect that I hear horror and stay silent.

Nurse

I beg of you, entreat you by your right hand,
your strong right hand, . . . don't speak of this!   605

Hippolytus

Don't lay your hand on me! Let go my cloak!

Nurse

By your knees then, . . . don't destroy me!

Hippolytus

What is this?
Don't you declare that you have done nothing wrong?

Nurse

Yes, but the story, son, is not for everyone.

Hippolytus

Why not? A pleasant tale makes pleasanter telling,
when there are many listeners.   610

Nurse

You will not break your oath to me, surely you will not?

Hippolytus

My tongue swore, but my mind was still unpledged.

Nurse

    Son, what would you do?
    You'll not destroy your friends?

Hippolytus

                   "Friends" you say!
    I spit the word away. None of the wicked
    are friends of mine.

Nurse

            Then pardon, son. It's natural
    that we should sin, being human.   615

Hippolytus

    Women! This coin which men find counterfeit!
    Why, why, Lord Zeus, did you put them in the world,
    in the light of the sun? If you were so determined
    to breed the race of man, the source of it
    should not have been women. Men might have dedicated
    in your own temples images of gold,   620
    silver, or weight of bronze, and thus have bought
    the seed of progeny, . . . to each been given
    his worth in sons according to the assessment
    of his gift's value. So we might have lived
    in houses free of the taint of women's presence.
    But now, to bring this plague into our homes   625
    we drain the fortunes of our homes. In this
    we have a proof how great a curse is woman.
    For the father who begets her, rears her up,
    must add a dowry gift to pack her off
    to another's house and thus be rid of the load.
    And he again that takes the cursed creature   630
    rejoices and enriches his heart's jewel
    with dear adornment, beauty heaped on vileness.
    With lovely clothes the poor wretch tricks her out
    spending the wealth that underprops his house.   635
    That husband has the easiest life whose wife
    is a mere nothingness, a simple fool,

uselessly sitting by the fireside.
I hate a clever woman—God forbid   640
that I should ever have a wife at home
with more than woman's wits! Lust breeds mischief
in the clever ones. The limits of their minds
deny the stupid lecherous delights.
We should not suffer servants to approach them,   645
but give them as companions voiceless beasts,
dumb, . . . but with teeth, that they might not converse,
and hear another voice in answer.
But now at home the mistress plots the mischief,
and the maid carries it abroad. So you, vile woman,   650
came here to me to bargain and to traffic
in the sanctity of my father's marriage bed.
I'll go to a running stream and pour its waters
into my ear to purge away the filth.
Shall I who cannot even hear such impurity,
and feel myself untouched, . . . shall I turn sinner?   655
Woman, know this. It is my piety saves you.
Had you not caught me off my guard and bound
my lips with an oath, by heaven I would not refrain
from telling this to my father.
Now I will go and leave this house until
Theseus returns from his foreign wanderings,
and I'll be silent. But I'll watch you close.   660
I'll walk with my father step by step and see
how you look at him, . . . you and your mistress both.
I have tasted of the daring of your infamy.
I'll know it for the future. Curses on you!
I'll hate you women, hate and hate and hate you,
and never have enough of hating. . . .
                                           Some
say that I talk of this eternally,   665
yes, but eternal, too, is woman's wickedness.
Either let someone teach them to be chaste,
or suffer me to trample on them forever.

(Phaedra comes out from behind the door. Exit Hippolytus.)

Phaedra

Bitter indeed is woman's destiny!
I have failed. What trick is there now, what cunning plea   670
to loose the knot around my neck?
I have had justice. O earth and the sunlight!
Where shall I escape from my fate?
How shall I hide my trouble?
What God or man would appear
to bear hand or part in my crime?   675
There is a limit to all suffering and I have reached it.
I am the unhappiest of women.

Chorus

Alas, mistress, all is over now   680
your servant's schemes have failed and you are ruined.

(Enter the Nurse.)

Phaedra

This is fine service you have rendered me,
corrupted, damned seducer of your friends!
May Zeus, the father of my fathers' line,
blot you out utterly, raze you from the world
with thunderbolts! Did I not see your purpose,   685
did I not say to you, "Breathe not a word of this"
which now overwhelms me with shame? But you,
you did not hold back. And therefore I must die
and die dishonored.
Enough of this. We have a new theme now.
The anger of Hippolytus is whetted.
He will tell his father all the story of your sin   690
to my disparagement. He will tell old Pittheus, too.
He will fill all the land with my dishonor.
May my curse
light upon you, on you and all the others
who eagerly help unwilling friends to ruin.

Nurse

    Mistress, you may well blame my ill-success,   695
    for sorrow's bite is master of your judgment.
    But I have an answer to make if you will listen.
    I reared you up. I am your loyal servant.
    I sought a remedy for your love's sickness,
    and found, . . . not what I sought.
    Had I succeeded, I had been a wise one.   700
    Our wisdom varies in proportion to
    our failure or achievement.

Phaedra

                         So, that's enough
    for me? Do I have justice if you deal me
    my death blow and then say "I was wrong: I grant it."

Nurse

    We talk too long. True I was not wise then.
    But even from this desperate plight, my child,   705
    you can escape.

Phaedra

                 You, speak no more to me.
    You have given me dishonorable advice.
    What you have tried has brought dishonor too.
    Away with you!
    Think of yourself. For me and my concerns
    I will arrange all well.

                               (Exit Nurse.)

    You noble ladies of Troezen, grant me this,   710
    this one request, that what you have heard here
    you wrap in silence.

Chorus Leader

    I swear by holy Artemis, child of Zeus,
    never to bring your troubles to the daylight.

Phaedra

    I thank you. I have found one single blessing   715
    in this unhappy business, one alone,

that I can pass on to my children after me
life with an uncontaminated name,
and myself profit by the present throw
of Fortune's dice. For I will never shame you,
my Cretan home, nor will I go to face
Theseus, defendant on an ugly charge,
never—for one life's sake.

Chorus Leader

What is the desperate deed you mean to do,
the deed past cure?

Phaedra

Death. But the way of it, that
is what I now must plan.

Chorus Leader

Oh, do not speak of it!

Phaedra

No, I'll not speak of it. But on this day
when I shake off the burden of this life
I shall delight the Goddess who destroys me,
the Goddess Cypris.
Bitter will have been the love that conquers me,
but in my death I shall at least bring sorrow,
upon another, too, that his high heart
may know no arrogant joy at my life's shipwreck;
he will have his share in this my mortal sickness
and learn of chastity in moderation.

Chorus

STROPHE

Would that I were under the cliffs, in the secret hiding-places of
    the rocks,
that Zeus might change me to a winged bird
and set me among the feathered flocks.
I would rise and fly to where the sea
washes the Adriatic coast,
and to the waters of Eridanus.

720

725

730

735

Into that deep-blue tide,
where their father, the Sun, goes down,
the unhappy maidens weep
tears from their amber-gleaming eyes   740
in pity for Phaethon.

ANTISTROPHE

I would win my way to the coast,
apple-bearing Hesperian coast,
of which the minstrels sing.
Where the Lord of the Ocean
denies the voyager further sailing,   745
and fixes the solemn limit of Heaven
which Giant Atlas upholds.
There the streams flow with ambrosia
by Zeus's bed of love,
and holy earth, the giver of life,   750
yields to the Gods rich blessedness.

STROPHE

O Cretan ship with the white sails,
from a happy home you brought her,
my mistress over the tossing foam, over the salty sea, 755
to bless her with a marriage unblest.
Black was the omen that sped her here,
black was the omen for both her lands,
for glorious Athens and her Cretan home,
as they bound to Munychia's pier   760
the cables' ends with their twisted strands
and stepped ashore on the continent.

ANTISTROPHE

The presage of the omen was true;   765
Aphrodite has broken her spirit
with the terrible sickness of impious love.
The waves of destruction are over her head,
from the roof of her room with its marriage bed,

she is tying the twisted noose.   770
And now it is around her fair white neck!
The shame of her cruel fate has conquered.
She has chosen good name rather than life:
she is easing her heart of its bitter load of love.   775

Nurse (*within*)

Ho, there, help!
You who are near the palace, help!
My mistress, Theseus' wife, has hanged herself.

Chorus Leader

It is done, she is hanged in the dangling rope.
Our Queen is dead.

Nurse (*within*)

Quick! Someone bring a knife!   780
Help me cut the knot around her neck.

                          (*The Chorus talks among itself.*)

First Woman

What shall we do, friends? Shall we cross the threshold,
and take the Queen from the grip of the tight-drawn cords?

Second Woman

Why should we? There are servants enough within
for that. Where hands are overbusy,
there is no safety.   785

Nurse (*within*)

Lay her out straight, poor lady.
Bitter shall my lord find her housekeeping.

Third Woman

From what I hear, the queen is dead.
They are already laying out the corpse.

SCENE IV

                          (*Theseus enters.*)

Theseus

Women, what is this crying in the house?   790

« 269 »

I heard heavy wailing on the wind,
as it were servants, mourning. And my house
deigns me no kindly welcome, though I come
crowned with good luck from Delphi.
The doors are shut against me. Can it be
something has happened to my father. He is old.   795
His life has traveled a great journey,
but bitter would be his passing from our house.

Chorus Leader

King, it is not the old who claim your sorrow.
Young is the dead and bitterly you'll grieve.

Theseus

My children . . . has death snatched a life away?

Chorus Leader

Your children live—but sorrowfully, King.   800
Their mother is dead.

Theseus

             It cannot be true, it cannot.
My wife! How could she be dead?

Chorus Leader

She herself tied the rope around her neck.

Theseus

Was it grief and numbing loneliness drove her to it,
or has there been some violence at work?

Chorus Leader

I know no more than this. I, too, came lately
to mourn for you and yours, King Theseus.   805

Theseus

Oh,
Why did I plait this coronal of leaves,
and crown my head with garlands, I the envoy
who find my journey end in misery.

(To the servants within.)

Open the doors! Unbar the fastenings,
that I may see this bitter sight, my wife
who killed me in her own death.   810

    *(The doors are opened, and Theseus goes inside. The Chorus in
        the Orchestra divide again into half-choruses and chant.)*

First Half-chorus

Woman unhappy, tortured,
your suffering, your death,
has shaken this house to its foundations.

Second Half-chorus

You were daring, you who died
in violence and guilt.
Here was a wrestling: your own hand against your life.   815

Chorus (united)

Who can have cast a shadow on your life?

<h2 style="text-align:center">Scene V</h2>

(Enter Theseus.)

Theseus

O city, city! Bitterness of sorrow!
Extremest sorrow that a man can suffer!
Fate, you have ground me and my house to dust,
fate in the form of some ineffable
pollution, some grim spirit of revenge.   820
The file has whittled away my life until
it is a life no more.
I am like a swimmer that falls into a great sea:
I cannot cross this towering wave I see before me.   825

My wife! I cannot think
of anything said or done to drive you to this horrible death.
You are like a bird that has vanished out of my hand.
You have made a quick leap out of my arms
into the land of Death.

It must be the sin of some of my ancestors in the dim past   830
God in his vengeance makes me pay now.

Chorus Leader

You are not the only one, King.
Many another as well as you
has lost a noble wife.   835

Theseus

Darkness beneath the earth, darkness beneath the earth!
How good to lie there and be dead,
now that I have lost you, my dearest comrade.
Your death is no less mine.   840
Will any of you
tell me what happened?
Or does the palace keep a flock of you for nothing?

God, the pain I saw in the house!
I cannot speak of it, I cannot bear it.   845
I cannot speak of it, I cannot bear it. I am a dead man.
My house is empty and my children orphaned.
You have left them, you
my loving wife—
the best of wives   850
of all the sun looks down on or the blazing stars of the night.

Chorus

Woe for the house! Such storms of ill assail it.
My eyes are wells of tears and overrun,
and still I fear the evil that shall come.   855

Theseus

Let her be, let her be:
What is this tablet fastened to her dear hand?
What can she wish to tell me of news?
Have you written begging me to care
for our children or, in entreaty,
about another woman? Sad one, rest confident.   860
There is no woman in the world who shall come to this house

and sleep by my side.
Look, the familiar signet ring,
hers who was once my wife!
Come, I will break the seals,
and see what this letter has to tell me.   865

(The Chorus of women speak singly.)

First Woman

Surely some God
brings sorrow upon sorrow in succession.

Second Woman

The house of our lords is destroyed: it is no more.   870

Third Woman

God, if it so may be, hear my prayer.
Do not destroy this house utterly. I am a prophet:
I can see the omen of coming trouble.

Theseus

Alas, here is endless sorrow upon sorrow.
It passes speech, passes endurance.   875

Chorus Leader

What is it? Tell us if we may share the story.

Theseus

It cries aloud, this tablet, cries aloud,
and Death is its song!   880

Chorus Leader

Prelude of ruin!

Theseus

I shall no longer hold this secret prisoner
in the gates of my mouth. It is horrible,
yet I will speak.
Citizens,
Hippolytus has dared to rape my wife.   885
He has dishonored God's holy sunlight.

(He turns in the direction of the sea.)

Father Poseidon, once you gave to me
three curses. . . . Now with one of these, I pray,
kill my son. Suffer him not to escape,
this very day, if you have promised truly.   890

Chorus Leader

Call back your curses, King, call back your curses.
Else you will realize that you were wrong
another day, too late. I pray you, trust me.

Theseus

I will not. And I now make this addition:
I banish him from this land's boundaries.
So fate shall strike him, one way or the other,
either Poseidon will respect my curse,   895
and send him dead into the House of Hades,
or exiled from this land, a beggar wandering,
on foreign soil, his life shall suck the dregs
of sorrow's cup.

Chorus Leader

Here comes your son, and seasonably, King Theseus.
Give over your deadly anger. You will best   900
determine for the welfare of your house.

                    (*Enter Hippolytus with companions.*)

Hippolytus

I heard you crying, father, and came quickly.
I know no cause why you should mourn.
Tell me.
                    (*Suddenly he sees the body of Phaedra.*)
O father, father—Phaedra! Dead! She's dead!   905
I cannot believe it. But a few moments since
I left her. . . . And she is still so young.
But what could it be? How did she die, father?
I *must* hear the truth from you. You say nothing to me?   910

When you are in trouble is no time for silence
The heart that would hear everything

is proved most greedy in misfortune's hour.
You should not hide your troubles from your friends,
and, father, those who are closer than your friends.   915

Theseus

What fools men are! You work and work for nothing,
you teach ten thousand tasks to one another,
invent, discover everything. One thing only
you do not know: one thing you never hunt for—
a way to teach fools wisdom.   920

Hippolytus

Clever indeed
would be the teacher able to compel
the stupid to be wise! This is no time
for such fine logic chopping.
                                        I am afraid
your tongue runs wild through sorrow.

Theseus

                                        If there were
some token now, some mark to make the division   925
clear between friend and friend, the true and the false!
All men should have two voices, one the just voice,
and one as chance would have it. In this way
the treacherous scheming voice would be confuted   930
by the just, and we should never be deceived.

Hippolytus

Some friend has poisoned your ear with slanderous tales.
Am I suspected, then, for all my innocence?
I am amazed. I am amazed to hear
your words. They are distraught. They go indeed
far wide of the mark!   935

Theseus

The mind of man—how far will it advance?
Where will its daring impudence find limits?
If human villainy and human life

shall wax in due proportion, if the son
shall always grow in wickedness past his father,
the Gods must add another world to this   940
that all the sinners may have space enough.

Look at this man! He was my son and he
dishonors my wife's bed! By the dead's testimony
he's clearly proved the vilest, falsest wretch.   945
Come—you could stain your conscience with the impurity—
show me your face; show it to me, your father.

You are the veritable holy man!
You walked with Gods in chastity immaculate!
I'll not believe your boasts of God's companionship: 950
the Gods are not so simple nor so ignorant.
Go, boast that you eat no meat, that you have Orpheus
for your king. Read until you are demented
your great thick books whose substance is as smoke.
For I have found you out. I tell you all,   955
avoid such men as he. They hunt their prey
with holy-seeming words, but their designs
are black and ugly. "She is dead," you thought,
"and that will save me." Fool, it is chiefly that
which proves your guilt. What oath that you can swear,   960
what speech that you can make for your acquittal,
outweighs this letter of hers? You'll say, to be sure,
she was your enemy and that the bastard son
is always hateful to the legitimate line.
Your words would argue her a foolish merchant
whose stock of merchandise was her own life
if she should throw away what she held dearest
to gratify her enmity for you.   965

Or you will tell me that this frantic folly
is inborn in a woman's nature; man
is different: but I know that young men
are no more to be trusted than a woman

when love disturbs the youthful blood in them.
The very male in them will make them false.   970
But why should I debate against you in words?
Here is the dead, surest of witnesses.
Get from this land with all the speed you can
to exile—may you rot there! Never again
come to our city, God-built Athens, nor
to countries over which my spear is king.   975

If I should take this injury at your hands
and pardon you, then Sinis of the Isthmus,
whom once I killed, would vow I never killed him,
but only bragged of the deed. And Sciron's rocks
washed by the sea would call me liar when
I swore I was a terror to ill-doers.   980

Chorus Leader

I cannot say of any man: he is happy.
See here how former happiness lies uprooted!

Hippolytus

Your mind and intellect are subtle, father:
here you have a subject dressed in eloquent words;
but if you lay the matter bare of words,   985
the matter is not eloquent. I am
no man to speak with vapid, precious skill
before a mob, although among my equals
and in a narrow circle I am held
not unaccomplished in the eloquent art.
That is as it should be. The demagogue
who charms a crowd is scorned by cultured experts.
But here in this necessity I must speak.   990
First I shall take the argument you first
urged as so irrefutable and deadly.
You see the earth and air about you, father?
In all of that there lives no man more chaste
than I, though you deny it.   995

« 277 »

It is my rule to honor the Gods first
and then to have as friends only such men
as do no sin, nor offer wicked service,
nor will consent to sin to serve a friend
as a return for kindness. I am no railer
at my companions. Those who are my friends   1000
find me as much their friends when they are absent
as when we are together.

There is one thing that I have never done, the thing
of which you think that you convict me, father,
I am a virgin to this very day.
Save what I have heard or what I have seen in pictures,   1005
I'm ignorant of the deed. Nor do I wish
to see such things, for I've a maiden soul.
But say you disbelieve my chastity.
Then tell me how it was *your* wife seduced me:
was it because she was more beautiful
than all the other women in the world?   1010
Or did I think, when I had taken her,
to win your place and kingdom for a dowry
and live in your own house? I would have been
a fool, a senseless fool, if I had dreamed it.
Was rule so sweet? Never, I tell you, Theseus,
for the wise. A man whom power has so enchanted
must be demented. I would wish to be   1015
first in the contests of the Greeks,
but in the city I'd take second place
and an enduring happy life among
the best society who are my friends.
So one has time to work, and danger's absence
has charms above the royal diadem.   1020
But a word more and my defense is finished.
If I had one more witness to my character,
if I were tried when *she* still saw the light,
deeds would have helped you as you scanned your friends

to know the true from the false. But now I swear,
I swear to you by Zeus, the God of oaths,   1025
by this deep-rooted fundament of earth,
I never sinned against you with your wife
nor would have wished or thought of it.
If I have been a villain, may I die
unfamed, unknown, a homeless stateless beggar,
an exile! May the earth and sea refuse   1030
to give my body rest when I am dead!
Whether your wife took her own life because
she was afraid, I do not know. I may not speak
further than this.
Virtuous she was in deed, although not virtuous:
I that have virtue used it to my ruin.   1035

Chorus Leader

You have rebutted the charge enough by your oath:
it is a great pledge you took in the God's name.

Theseus

Why, here's a spell-binding magician for you!
He wrongs his father and then trusts his craft,
his smooth beguiling craft to lull my anger.   1040

Hippolytus

Father, I must wonder at this in you.
If I were father now, and you were son,
I would not have banished you to exile! I
would have killed you if I thought you touched my wife.

Theseus

This speech is worthy of you: but you'll not die so.   1045
A quick death is the easiest of ends
for miserable men. No, you'll go wandering
far from your fatherland and beg your way.
This is the payment of the impious man.   1050

Hippolytus

What will you do? You will not wait until

time's pointing finger proves me innocent.
Must I go at once to banishment?

Theseus

                         Yes, and had I the power,
your place of banishment would be beyond
the limits of the world, the encircling sea
and the Atlantic Pillars.
That is the measure of my hate, my son.

Hippolytus

Pledges, oaths, and oracles—you will not test them?   1055
You will banish me from the kingdom without trial?

Theseus

This letter here is proof without lot-casting.
The ominous birds may fly above my head:
they do not trouble me.

Hippolytus

                   Eternal Gods!
Dare I speak out, since I am ruined now   1060
through loyalty to the oath I took by you?
No, he would not believe who should believe
and I should be false to my oath for nothing.

Theseus

This is more of your holy juggling!
I cannot stomach it. Away with you!
Get from this country—and go quickly!   1065

Hippolytus

Where shall I turn? What friend will take me in,
when I am banished on a charge like this?

Theseus

Doubtless some man who loves to entertain
his wife's seducers welcoming them at the hearth.

Hippolytus

That blow went home.   1070

I am near crying when I think that I
am judged to be guilty and that it is you who are judge.

Theseus

You might have sobbed and snivelled long ago,
and thought of that before when you resolved
to rape your father's wife.

Hippolytus

House, speak for me!
Take voice and bear me witness if I have sinned.   1075

Theseus

You have a clever trick of citing witnesses,
whose testimony is dumb. Here is your handiwork.

(*Points to the body.*)

It, too, can't speak—but it convicts you.

Hippolytus

If I could only find
another *me* to look me in the face
and see my tears and all that I am suffering!

Theseus

Yes, in self-worship you are certainly practiced.   1080
You are more at home there than in the other virtues,
justice, for instance, and duty toward a father.

Hippolytus

Unhappy mother mine, and bitter birth-pangs,
when you gave me to the world! I would not wish
on any of my friends a bastard's birth.

Theseus (to the servants)

Drag him away!
Did you not hear me, men, a long time since
proclaiming his decree of banishment?   1085

Hippolytus

Let one of them touch me at his peril! But you,
you drive me out yourself—if you have the heart!

Theseus

    I'll do it, too, unless you go at once.
    No, there is no chance that pity for your exile
    will steal on my hard heart and make me change.

                  (Theseus goes out.)

Hippolytus

    So, I'm condemned and there is no release.   1090
    I know the truth and dare not tell the truth.

            (He turns to the statue of Artemis.)

    Daughter of Leto, dearest of the Gods to me,
    comrade and partner in the hunt, behold me,
    banished from famous Athens.
    Farewell, city! Farewell Erechtheus' land!   1095
    Troezen, farewell! So many happy times
    you knew to give a young man, growing up.
    This is the last time I shall look upon you,
    the last time I shall greet you.

                  (To his companions.)

    Come friends, you are of my age and of this country,
    say your farewells and set me on my way.
    You will not see a man more innocent—   1100
    innocent despite my judge!—condemned to banishment.

                (Hippolytus goes out.)

Chorus

STROPHE

    The care of God for us is a great thing,
    if a man believe it at heart:
    it plucks the burden of sorrow from him.
    So I have a secret hope   1105
    of someone, a God, who is wise and plans;
    but my hopes grow dim when I see
    the deeds of men and their destinies.

    For fortune is ever veering, and the currents of life are shifting
    shifting, wandering forever.   1110

Antistrophe

This is the lot in life I seek
and I pray that God may grant it me,
luck and prosperity
and a heart untroubled by anguish.
And a mind that is neither false clipped coin,
nor too clear-eyed in sincerity,
that I may lightly change my ways,
my ways of today when tomorrow comes,
and so be happy all my life long.

1115

Strophe

My heart is no longer clear:
I have seen what I never dreamed,
I have seen the brightest star of Athens,
stricken by a father's wrath,
banished to an alien land.

1120

1125

Sands of the seashore!
Thicket of the mountain!
Where with his pacing hounds
he hunted wild beasts and killed
to the honor of holy Dictynna.

1130

Antistrophe

He will never again mount his car
with its span of Venetian mares,
nor fill the ring of Limnae with the sound of horses' hoofs.
The music which never slept
on the strings of his lyre, shall be dumb,
shall be dumb in his father's house.
The haunts of the Goddess Maid
in the deep rich meadow shall want their crowns.
You are banished: there's an end
of the rivalry of maids for your love.

1135

1140

EPODE

But my sorrow shall not die,
still my eyes shall be wet with tears
for your heartless doom.
Sad mother, you bore him in vain:　　　　　　　　1145
I am angry against the Gods.
Sister Graces, why did you let him go
guiltless, out of his native land,
out of his father's house?　　　　　　　　　　1150

But here I see Hippolytus' servant,
in haste making for the house, his face sorrowful.

SCENE VI

(Enter a Messenger.)

Messenger

Where shall I go to find King Theseus, women?
If you know, tell me. Is he within doors?　　　　1155

Chorus

Here he is coming out.

Messenger

King Theseus,
I bring you news worthy of much thought
for you and all the citizens who live
in Athens' walls and boundaries of Troezen.

Theseus

What is it? Has some still newer disaster　　　　1160
seized my two neighboring cities?

Messenger

Hippolytus is dead: I may almost say dead:
he sees the light of day still, though the balance
that holds him in this world is slight indeed.

Theseus

Who killed him? I can guess that someone hated him,
whose wife he raped, as he did mine, his father's.　　1165

Messenger

> It was the horses of his own car that killed him,
> they, and the curses of your lips,
> the curses you invoked against your son,
> and prayed the Lord of Ocean to fulfil them.

Theseus

> O Gods—Poseidon, you are then truly
> my father! You have heard my prayers.   1170
> How did he die? Tell me. How did the beam
> of Justice's dead-fall strike him, my dishonorer?

Messenger

> We were combing our horses' coats beside the sea,
> where the waves came crashing to the shore. And we were crying
> for one had come and told us that our master,   1175
> Hippolytus, should walk this land no more,
> since you had laid hard banishment upon him.
> Then he came himself down to the shore to us,
> with the same refrain of tears,
> and with him walked a countless company
> of friends and young men his own age.   1180
>
> But at last he gave over crying and said:
> Why do I rave like this? It is my father
> who has commanded and I must obey him.
> Prepare my horses, men, and harness them.
> There is no longer a city of mine.
> Then every man made haste. Before you could say the words,   1185
> there was the chariot ready before our master.
> He put his feet into the driver's rings,
> and took the reins from the rail into his hands.
> But first he folded his hands like this and prayed: 1190
> Zeus, let me die now, if I have been guilty!
> Let my father know that he has done me wrong,
> whether I live to see the day or not.
>
> With that, he took the goad and touched the horses.
> And we his servants followed our master's car,   1195

close by the horses' heads, on the straight road
that leads to Argos and to Epidaurus.
When we were entering the lonely country
the other side of the border, where the shore   1200
goes down to the Saronic Gulf, a rumbling
deep in the earth, terrible to hear,
growled like the thunder of Father Zeus.
The horses raised their heads, pricked up their ears,
and gusty fear was on us all to know,
whence came the sound. As we looked toward the shore,   1205
where the waves were beating, we saw a wave appear,
a miracle wave, lifting its crest to the sky,
so high that Sciron's coast was blotted out
from my eye's vision. And it hid the Isthmus
and the Asclepius Rock. To the shore it came,   1210
swelling, boiling, crashing, casting its surf around,
to where the chariot stood.
But at the very moment when it broke,
the wave threw up a monstrous savage bull.
Its bellowing filled the land, and the land echoed it,   1215
with shuddering emphasis. And sudden panic
fell on the horses in the car. But the master—
he was used to horses' ways—all his life long
he had been with horses—took a firm grip of the reins   1220
and lashed the ends behind his back and pulled
like a sailor at the oar. The horses bolted:
their teeth were clenched upon the fire-forged bit.
They heeded neither the driver's hand nor harness
nor the jointed car. As often as he would turn them   1225
with guiding hand to the soft sand of the shore,
the bull appeared in front to head them off,
maddening the team with terror.
But when in frenzy they charged toward the cliffs,   1230
the bull came galloping beside the rail,
silently following until he brought disaster,
capsizing the car, striking the wheel on a rock.

Then all was in confusion. Axles of wheels,
and lynch-pins flew up into the air,   1235
and he the unlucky driver, tangled in the reins,
was dragged along in an inextricable
knot, and his dear head pounded on the rocks,
his body bruised. He cried aloud and terrible
his voice rang in our ears: Stand, horses, stand!   1240
You were fed in my stables. Do not kill me!
My father's curse! His curse! Will none of you
save me? I am innocent. Save me!

Many of us had will enough, but all
were left behind in the race. Getting free of the reins,
somehow he fell. There was still life in him.   1245
But the horses vanished and that ill-omened monster,
somewhere, I know not where, in the rough cliffs.

I am only a slave in your household, King Theseus,
but I shall never be able to believe   1250
that your son was guilty, not though the tribe of women
were hanged for it, not though the weight of tablets
of a high pine of Ida, filled with writing,
accused him—for I know that he was good.

Chorus Leader

It has been fulfilled, this bitter, new disaster,   1255
for what is doomed and fated there is no quittance.

Theseus

For hatred of the sufferer I was glad
at what you told me. Still, he was my son.
As such I have reverence for him and the Gods:
I neither rejoice nor sorrow at this thing.   1260

Messenger

What is your pleasure that we do with him?
Would you have him brought to you? If I might counsel,
you would not be harsh with your son—now he is unfortunate.

Theseus

    Bring him to me that I may see his face.   1265

    He swore that he had never wronged my wife.

    I will refute him with God's punishing stroke.

Chorus

    Cypris, you guide men's hearts

    and the inflexible

    hearts of the Gods and with you

    comes Love with the flashing wings,   1270

    comes Love with the swiftest of wings.

    Over the earth he flies

    and the loud-echoing salt-sea.

    He bewitches and maddens the heart

    of the victim he swoops upon.   1275

    He bewitches the race of the mountain-hunting

    lions and beasts of the sea,

    and all the creatures that earth feeds,

    and the blazing sun sees—

    and man, too—

    over all you hold kingly power,   1280

    Love, you are only ruler

    over all these.

EPILOGUE

Artemis

    I call on the noble king, the son of Aegeus,

    to hear me! It is I, Artemis, child of Leto.   1285

    Miserable man, what joy have you in this?

    You have murdered a son, you have broken nature's laws.

    Dark indeed was the conclusion

    you drew from your wife's lying accusations,

    but plain for all to see is the destruction

    to which they led you.

    There is a hell beneath the earth: haste to it,   1290

    and hide your head there! Or will you take wings,

and choosing the life of a bird instead of man
keep your feet from destruction's path in which they tread?
Among good men, at least, you have no share in life.   1295
Hear me tell you, Theseus, how these things came to pass.
I shall not better them, but I will give you pain.
I have come here for this—to show you that your son's heart
was always just, so just that for his good name
he endured to die. I will show you, too,
the frenzied love that seized your wife, or I may call it,   1300
a noble innocence. For that most hated Goddess,
hated by all of us whose joy is virginity,
drove her with love's sharp prickings to desire
your son. She tried to overcome her love
with the mind's power, but at last against her will,
she fell by the nurse's strategems,   1305
the nurse, who told your son under oath her mistress loved him.
But he, just man, did not fall in with her
counsels, and even when reviled by you
refused to break the oath he had pledged.
Such was his piety. But your wife fearing
lest she be proved the sinner wrote a letter,   1310
a letter full of lies; and so she killed
your son by treachery; but she convinced you.

Theseus

Alas!

Artemis

This is a bitter story, Theseus. Stay,
hear more that you may groan the more.
You know you had three curses from your father,   1315
three, clear for you to use? One you have launched,
vile wretch, at your own son, when you might have
spent it upon an enemy. Your father,
King of the Sea, in loving kindness to you
gave you, by his bequest, all that he ought.
But you've been proved at fault both in his eyes   1320

and mine in that you did not stay for oaths
nor voice of oracles, nor gave a thought
to what time might have shown; only too quickly
you hurled the curses at your son and killed him.

Theseus

Mistress, I am destroyed.

Artemis

You have sinned indeed, but yet you may win pardon.   1325
For it was Cypris managed the thing this way
to gratify her anger against Hippolytus.
This is the settled custom of the Gods:
No one may fly in the face of another's wish:
we remain aloof and neutral. Else, I assure you,   1330
had I not feared Zeus, I never would have endured
such shame as this—my best friend among men
killed, and I could do nothing.
As for you, in the first place ignorance acquits you,
and then your wife, by her death, destroyed the proofs,   1335
the verbal proofs which might have still convinced you.
You and I are the chief sufferers, Theseus.
Misfortune for you, grief for me.
The Gods do not rejoice when pious worshippers die: 1340
the wicked we destroy, children, house and all.

Chorus

Here comes the suffering Hippolytus,
his fair young body and his golden head,
a battered wreck. O trouble of the house,
what double sorrow from the hand of God   1345
has been fulfilled for this our royal palace!

Hippolytus

A battered wreck of body! Unjust father,
and oracle unjust—this is your work.
Woe for my fate!   1350
My head is filled with shooting agony,

and in my brain there is a leaping fire.
Let me be!
For I would rest my weary frame awhile.
Curse on my team! How often have I fed you   1355
from my own hand, you who have murdered me!
O, O!
In God's name touch my wounded body gently.
Who is this standing on the right of me?   1360
Come lift me carefully, bear me easily,
a man unlucky, cursed by my own father
in bitter error. Zeus, do you see this,
see me that worshipped God in piety,   1365
me that excelled all men in chastity,
see me now go to death which gapes before me;
all my life lost, and all for nothing now
labors of piety in the face of men?

O the pain, the pain that comes upon me!   1370
Let me be, let me be, you wretches!
May death the healer come for me at last!
You kill me ten times over with this pain.
O for a spear with a keen cutting edge   1375
to shear me apart—and give me my last sleep!
Father, your deadly curse!
This evil comes from some manslaying of old,   1380
some ancient tale of murder among my kin.
But why should it strike me, who am clear of guilt?
What is there to say? How can I shake from me   1385
this pitiless pain? O death, black night of death,
resistless death, come to me now the miserable,
and give me sleep!

Artemis

Unhappy boy! You are yoked to a cruel fate.
The nobility of your soul has proved your ruin.   1390

Hippolytus

O divine fragrance! Even in my pain

I sense it, and the suffering is lightened.
The Goddess Artemis is near this place.

Artemis

She is, the dearest of the Gods to you.

Hippolytus

You see my suffering, mistress?   1395

Artemis

I see it. Heavenly law forbids my tears.

Hippolytus

Gone is your huntsman, gone your servant now.

Artemis

Yes, truly: but you die beloved by me.

Hippolytus

Gone is your groom, gone your shrine's guardian.

Artemis

Cypris, the worker of mischief, so contrived.   1400

Hippolytus

Alas, I know the Goddess who destroyed me!

Artemis

She blamed your disrespect, hated your chastity.

Hippolytus

She claimed us three as victims then, did Cypris?

Artemis

Your father, you, and me to make a third.

Hippolytus

Yes, I am sorry for my father's suffering.   1405

Artemis

Cypris deceived him by her cunning snares.

Hippolytus

O father, this is sorrow for you indeed!

Theseus

    I, too, am dead now. I have no more joy in life.

Hippolytus

    I sorrow for you in this more than myself.

Theseus

    Would that it was I who was dying instead of you!   1410

Hippolytus

    Bitter were Poseidon's gifts, my father, bitter.

Theseus

    Would that they had never come into my mouth.

Hippolytus

    Even without them, you would have killed me—
    you were so angry.

Theseus

                A God tripped up my judgment.

Hippolytus

    O, if only men might be a curse to Gods!   1415

Artemis

    Hush, that is enough! You shall not be unavenged,
    Cypris shall find the angry shafts she hurled
    against you for your piety and innocence
    shall cost her dear.
    I'll wait until she loves a mortal next time,   1420
    and with this hand—with these unerring arrows
    I'll punish him.

    To you, unfortunate Hippolytus,
    by way of compensation for these ills,
    I will give the greatest honors of Troezen.
    Unwedded maids before the day of marriage   1425
    will cut their hair in your honor. You will reap
    through the long cycle of time, a rich reward in tears.
    And when young girls sing songs, they will not forget you,

your name will not be left unmentioned,
nor Phaedra's love for you remain unsung.   1430

(*To Theseus.*)

Son of old Aegeus, take your son
to your embrace. Draw him to you. Unknowing
you killed him. It is natural for men
to err when they are blinded by the Gods.

(*To Hippolytus.*)

Do not bear a grudge against your father.   1435
It was fate that you should die so.
Farewell, I must not look upon the dead.
My eye must not be polluted by the last
gaspings for breath. I see you are near this.

Hippolytus

Farewell to you, too holy maiden! Go in peace.   1440
You can lightly leave a long companionship.
You bid me end my quarrel with my father,
and I obey. In the past, too, I obeyed you.

The darkness is upon my eyes already.

Father, lay hold on me and lift me up.   1445

Theseus

Alas, what are you doing to me, my son?

Hippolytus

I am dying. I can see the gates of death.

Theseus

And so you leave me, my hands stained with murder.

Hippolytus

No, for I free you from all guilt in this.

Theseus

You will acquit me of blood guiltiness?   1450

Hippolytus

So help me Artemis of the conquering bow!

Theseus

Dear son, how noble you have proved to me!

Hippolytus

Yes, pray to heaven for such legitimate sons.

Theseus

Woe for your goodness, piety, and virtue.

Hippolytus

Farewell to you, too, father, a long farewell!　　　　　1455

Theseus

Dear son, bear up. Do not forsake me.

Hippolytus

This is the end of what I have to bear.
I'm gone. Cover my face up quickly.

Theseus

Pallas Athene's famous city,
what a man you have lost! Alas for me!　　　　　1460
Cypris, how many of your injuries
I shall remember.

Chorus

This is a common grief for all the city;
it came unlooked for. There shall be
a storm of multitudinous tears for this;
the lamentable stories of great men　　　　　1465
prevail more than of humble folk.

THE COMPLETE GREEK TRAGEDIES

AESCHYLUS · I *ORESTEIA*

Translated and with an Introduction by Richmond Lattimore

Agamemnon
The Libation Bearers
The Eumenides

AESCHYLUS · II *FOUR TRAGEDIES*

The Suppliant Maidens. *S. G. Benardete*
The Persians. *S. G. Benardete*
Seven against Thebes. *David Grene*
Prometheus Bound. *David Grene*

SOPHOCLES · I *THREE TRAGEDIES*

Translated and with an Introduction by David Grene

Oedipus the King
Oedipus at Colonus
Antigone

SOPHOCLES · II *FOUR TRAGEDIES*

Ajax. *John Moore*
The Women of Trachis. *Michael Jameson*
Electra *and* Philoctetes. *David Grene*

EURIPIDES · I *FOUR TRAGEDIES*

With an Introduction by Richmond Lattimore

Alcestis. *Richmond Lattimore*
The Medea. *Rex Warner*
The Heracleidae. *Ralph Gladstone*
Hippolytus. *David Grene*

EURIPIDES · II *FOUR TRAGEDIES*

The Cyclops *and* Heracles. *William Arrowsmith*
Iphigenia in Tauris. *Witter Bynner. Introduction by Richmond Lattimore*
Helen. *Richmond Lattimore*

EURIPIDES · III *FOUR TRAGEDIES*

Hecuba. *William Arrowsmith*
Andromache. *John Frederick Nims*
The Trojan Women. *Richmond Lattimore*
Ion. *R. F. Willetts*

EURIPIDES · IV *FOUR TRAGEDIES*

Rhesus. *Richmond Lattimore*
The Suppliant Women. *Frank William Jones*
Orestes. *William Arrowsmith*
Iphigenia in Aulis. *Charles R. Walker*

EURIPIDES · V *THREE TRAGEDIES*

Electra. *Emily Townsend Vermeule*
The Phoenician Women. *Elizabeth Wyckoff*
The Bacchae. *William Arrowsmith*